ENGLAND, BLOODY ENGLAND

AN EXPATRIATE'S RETURN

LESLEY HAZLETON

THE ATLANTIC MONTHLY PRESS
NEW YORK

Portions of this book have appeared, in slightly different form, in *The New York Times*, *Tikkun*, *Lear's*, and *Arete*.

Published simultaneously in Canada
Printed in the United States of America

Library of Congress Cataloging-in-Publication Data
Hazleton, Lesley.
  England, bloody England: an expatriate's return / Lesley
  Hazleton.
  ISBN 0-87113-329-6
  1. England—Description and travel—1971– 2. Hazleton, Lesley—
  Journeys—England. I. Title.
DA632.H39   1990   914.204'858—dc20   89-6923

Design by Laura Hough

The Atlantic Monthly Press
19 Union Square West
New York, NY 10003

FIRST PRINTING

For my grandmother, Esther

I was never very good at being English. I was born in England, to be sure, and bred there. I lived there the first twenty years of my life. But still, something was missing. Some little link that seemed peculiarly elusive. Some trick that evaded me, like a child who knows a conjuror is faking it, but can't tell how. It was as though I were a foreigner speaking the language so well that no other foreigner would imagine I didn't really belong. Only those on the inside would know, and then only by the most subtle of signs—so subtle, it seemed, even Claude Lévi-Strauss would be hard put to detect them.

When I left England, fresh out of university, it felt like an escape. I was relieved of the burden of trying to be English. Eventually, I moved to the United States, and my accent became mid-Atlantic. I sounded English to Americans, and American to the English. And on trips back to England, on journalistic assignment or to see my family, I discovered an unexpected bonus—the more the English thought me American, the easier it was for me to be there.

Ironically, being perceived as a foreigner gave me an unaccustomed freedom. The English made allowances for me. Together, we could flaunt the rules of civilized English communication; that is, we could talk directly. Which is how I found myself confessing to a newfound friend, over a gin and tonic in his London club, that I'd never quite gotten the knack of being English.

He sighed. "Oh, yes," he said. "We never say so, of course, but we all feel that way."

I stared in astonishment. He smiled a little sheepishly. "That's part of being English, isn't it?" he said.

I couldn't tell if the look in his eyes was ironic or sad. In retrospect, I think it must have been both.

DRY ROT

EARLY morning is the kindest time for a city in decay. The pale light, filtered through high clouds; the chill wind blowing off the Mersey; the echo of your footsteps on the cracked pavements; the international language of gulls wheeling on the air currents, not yet drowned out by the noises of day . . . These are the things that make decay romantic, at least to a nineteen-year-old. And the mists; above all, the mists. Sea mists rolling in from the Irish Sea, down the vast open estuary of the Mersey, up the hillside and over the bomb sites of Liverpool 8, a neighborhood so neglected that it never even had a name, just a number.

This was the north of England. Even then, twenty years ago, the abandoned north. It was less than three hundred miles from where I grew up, amidst the affluent greenery and impeccable gardens of the south. But in England three hundred miles leads you to another world.

Liverpool had once been a thriving port city, in the days when England was empress of the seas and the world's main naval and trading power. In the days of empire, that is. But those days were long gone, and the great divide between the north and the south of England was a divide of class and money. Liverpool was working class, and it was falling apart.

They were kind, those early morning mists. They hid the craters and the rubble, the rusted, abandoned cars and the meager, drooping attempts at market gardens. Twenty years after the end of the Second World War, they still hid its evidence, at least for an hour or two. And in Liverpool 8, you are grateful for even an hour or two of kindness.

Back then in the sixties, I seemed to spend more time in Liverpool than in Manchester, where I was at university. I'd stay overnight and leave early in the morning, bundled up in my student uniform of jeans and duffel coat and long striped university scarf draped in multiple loops around my neck. It was only ten minutes' walk to the main road leading out of Liverpool, the road to Manchester. As though teasing a whole city with impossible dreams, it was called the London Road. There I'd stick out my thumb, and shiver, and hope that a truck would come along in time for me to make my first lecture of the day in Manchester, an hour's drive to the east.

But on those mornings, I'd first wander down to the old cathedral, a huge Gothic brick pile that dominated the skyline, set between Liverpool 8 and the river, on the very edge of the hill. They were still building the new cathedral back then, the Roman Catholic one that nobody liked at the other end of Hope Street. It was a round, pale concrete structure, insistently modernistic and shaped like a crown of thorns. It had none of the comforting grandeur of the Anglican one. And it didn't have a moat.

The mist rose from the old cathedral's moat in long, wavering tendrils, reaching up into the early morning air as though to claim me, to envelop me and pull me down into the old graveyards at the bottom with their maze of broken gravestones and untended grass, abandoned condoms and old tin cans. Mist clung to the sides of the cathedral, set high on its hill surrounded by the moat. It licked the brickwork, embraced it, as though the spirits of those trapped in the miasma below were begging for mercy.

I would stand there, clinging to the railings, watching the mist shift shape and mass with the wind, staring past the cathedral tower down to the river and listening for the muffled, distant horn of the Liverpool-Birkenhead ferry as it set out on its first crossing of the day. The old Georgian terrace houses behind me seemed frail in their shabbiness, as though they'd long since given up all former claims to beauty and had resigned themselves to inexorably, slowly crumbling away.

The cathedral was on Hope Street. Off Hope Street ran Paradise Street, and Mount Pleasant Street, and Knight Street, and Pilgrim Street, and the Street of the Slough of Despond. As though this part of Liverpool 8 was a map of *The Pilgrim's Progress,* and I, clinging to the railings, was the pilgrim caught between Hope and the Slough of Despond.

"Hope Street," I'd repeat to myself, "Hope Street." As though if I said it enough times, there could be some hope in this landscape of decay.

It is true I spent most of my time in Liverpool stoned. It was the sixties, after all, and some of the docks were still working, and the grass that came in from Nigeria was the best of all, soft and sweet and fragrant. They were innocent times. There was a group of us, about seven or eight, and we'd walk through the streets holding joints cupped in the palms of our hands, working-man's style, to protect the lit end from the wind. We'd take the back row of the single movie house left in Liverpool 8, which showed splendidly lurid B movies, and there I watched Rasputin rise time and again from the dead through a fog of fragrant smoke. Students and dropouts, idealists and dreamers, we'd gather in the room of a poet friend, an attic room very like the one in Henry Wallis's painting of the dead Chatterton, except that through the windows we saw not the spires of Westminster and Saint Paul's, but the leaden gray skies of Merseyside, gentled by the magic plant from another, sunnier clime. We'd talk poetry and revolution—our cabbages and kings—and late at night when the others had gone, the poet and I would cling close to each other for warmth on the stark single bed.

But those early mornings, I wasn't stoned. I was wide awake and clear-eyed, as only a nineteen-year-old can be after nights like that. So why, twenty years later, did I remember so clearly the Street of the Slough of Despond? Because when I went back to find it, it wasn't there. And never had been.

Though God knows it should have been.

"DRY rot," says Ken Worrall. "That's the curse here. You know what the Latin name is? *Merulius Lacrymans.* That means crying river. Ironic, isn't it?"

Ken is an architect, an award-winning specialist in restoration and a one-man strike force in Liverpool 8's struggle for physical survival. When I decided to come up north and see the worsened north-south divide for myself, an old friend from those long-gone Liverpool days told me to contact Ken. "If you want to know what's happening in Liverpool," he said, "and how it's changed since we knew it, Ken's your man."

The moment I saw him, I knew that was true. Gaunt and gap toothed, clad in a well-worn leather bomber jacket, Ken has the look of a man who can handle himself as well on the streets as in the office. We hit it off quickly, and soon, over a pint or two of best bitter, he's telling me stories of floors he's stepped on and fallen straight through to the rooms below. Stories of physical decay.

Dry rot is a fungus. It spreads through damp walls to eat away floors, beams, joists, struts, any wood it can reach. It is epidemic in Liverpool 8. A house is abandoned, "the lads" move in and strip it, and it's open to the weather. Come the winter, the rains soak the walls so well that as the temperature rises towards summer, the fungus swells and attacks.

"Nobody cares," says Ken as he rolls himself a cigarette in licorice paper. He rolls it nice and easy, the way I remember doing it, the paper sweet between the lips and the tobacco strong in the mouth. "Nobody thinks. That's the problem. The marble fireplaces, they're always the first to go. All right, that's not so bad. You can get five hundred quid for a marble fireplace. But then the lads go up to the roof and strip the lead lining from the gutters.

6

What do they do that for? You get pennies for lead. A house can survive without a marble fireplace, but once you strip that lead lining . . ."

"The lads"—it's a good Liverpool term, friendly. It can mean anything from the friends you meet down at the pub to the gangs of out-of-work teenagers roaming the streets looking for heroin money. Here's a story of the lads in Liverpool 8:

Ken's house, an old Georgian terrace house that he's renovating slowly as he lives in it, has a garage in the back garden. The garage leads into a back alley. The doors are padlocked from the inside, but the window on the garden side has no glass in it. Ken doesn't own a car—"Who needs a car when you're five minutes' walk from the center of the city?" For some time, all he's kept in the garage is a big mound of sand. Which is why he was somewhat surprised when he walked in there one day to find a huge silver Mercedes—"The latest model, fuel injection, mahogany woodwork, all mod cons"—neatly parked over his sand. He called the police. The car, it turned out, had been stolen in Chester two days before.

He thought a bit and realized that this might be a tricky situation. Whoever stole the car would not be pleased to find it no longer there. So he wrote a note and pinned it to the frame of the glassless window. "Dear lads," it read, "I have to tell you that this house is lived in, so I came across the object you left here for safekeeping. Sorry lads, but I had to tell the police. Someone might have seen it come in. They took it away. However, I'm sure if you want it back, you'll find it at its original location within two or three days."

The next time he looked, the note had gone. To his relief, he heard nothing more about it.

You have to know the ropes to survive in Liverpool 8. Unemployment in some parts is close to seventy percent. "If you're white," says Ken, "it's really hard to find a job. If you're black, it's just about impossible." New housing developments have become slums inside twenty years, some of them boarded up and empty, not because there's nobody waiting to live there, but because of mismanagement by a militant-left city council that wreaked ideological havoc on the city in the late seventies and early eighties. Some of the old bomb sites were made into parks, but they soon became slightly greener versions of the originals— filthy, unkempt, full of refuse.

And then there are the burned-out sites from the riots—the Toxteth riots of 1981, the year it seemed all of England's inner cities were burning. The year the frustration and unemployment and hopelessness and teenage energy combined in a fury of rioting, looting, and destruction.

Toxteth is the neighborhood bordering Liverpool 8. The media probably came up with "the Toxteth riots" because "the Liverpool 8 riots" just doesn't roll off the tongue. Ken told me how he had watched, fascinated, as the lads battled the police.

"The police came up Parly Hill . . ."—that's Parliament Hill, abbreviated in the way everything familiar gets abbreviated in Liverpool, like "the Philly" for the Philharmonic pub, or "Seffy Park" for Sefton Park. "They were beating their clubs against their shields as they came up. Here, at the top of the hill, there's a petrol station on one side of the road, and a dairy on the other. Lots of petrol in the petrol station, and lots of empty bottles in the dairy . . ."

Molotov cocktails rained down on the police. A full-scale battle ensued.

"See that burned-out site there?" says Ken. "That's where the Racquets Club was. It used to be one of those exclusive nob places, all cigars and brandy. They picked that one out. Then this building here, next door, is a nursing home. They didn't touch that. Then here, on the other side, is where the Rialto was—that used to be the cinema, and then it got taken over by this furniture dealer. He was well known in the neighborhood. Used to buy up an old widow's home, all the contents, for five hundred quid, knowing all the time that he could sell any one of those old antiques for two or three thousand. Then he'd store them in the basement and ship them off to America, where he'd get even higher prices for them. Then on the main floor, he'd sell this cheap naugahyde furniture at inflated prices to the people who lived here. Everyone knew what he was up to. So they burned him out."

We turn in the direction of Toxteth. This street looks like Newark, New Jersey, after the sixties riots there. "They got out of control in this street," Ken admits. "Burned out small shopkeepers. Not rich men, just little stores that served the community. This is the only street where that happened."

And it was this one street that led to Margaret Thatcher's famous comment on the riots. "Oh, those poor shopkeepers," was all she had to say.

EVEN the Adelphi Hotel, the city's best and fanciest, is suffering. Its grand ballrooms and reception rooms have been reduced to tackiness under bad lighting and too many coats of hastily applied paint. In the marbled peristyle room, the pillars are carved into the shape of palm trees, but what should be exotic merely looks sad, pretensions betrayed by neglect.

My room reflects perfectly the shabby image of the traveling salesman's life, with drab brown wallpaper and an ancient steam radiator with the paint peeling off it, and in the corner, a tin tray set with an electric kettle, a cup and saucer, and little packets of tea, sugar, and powdered Carnation milk. None of the three light bulbs have more than sixty watts.

I switch on the evening news. Even the television commercials are different up here in the north:

"Come to the government job center, and we'll find you a job," says a young woman's bright voice over a picture of the job center. She has a southern accent, upper middle class. In the south, there are plenty of jobs to be found. Here, in Liverpool, it seems a cruel tease. There are no jobs here, and the upper class and upper middle class have long ago fled for greener pastures.

"Come see us at British Gas if you can't pay your gas bill, and we'll work out a way for you to pay it without us cutting off your supply," says another happy female voice, perhaps the same one.

"Drink Beecham's Hot Lemon for colds and snuffles," says a warm, reassuring northern voice, a man this time. He speaks over shots of a small, northern terrace-house room, a coal fire, a man and a woman damp and shivering and sneezing. Beecham's knows what life is like up north.

"Buy a television and video for only twelve pounds a month." Another man's voice, again a northern accent, but he makes no mention of how many months are involved.

"Go to sunny Majorca on an all-inclusive package holiday." The price flashes bright red again and again, teasing the northerner's imagination once more with those impossible palm trees.

None of these commercials show in the south, where admen work on affluent fantasies. There, everyone pays their gas bills and nobody gets colds. Only the working class go to Majorca.

On the news, Charles and Di are in Australia. Di is wilting in the heat and shooting I'll-get-you-later-for-this looks at Charles. Riot police are called out against nurses trying to march on Parliament, asking for a pay raise. A nurse weeps in frustration as she bangs her fist against a policeman's chest. The government is denying there was ever a shoot-to-kill policy in Northern Ireland. The Israelis are denying there is one in the West Bank. The Americans are denying any connection with Iran.

I call my parents after the news. "Good lord, the Adelphi," says my mother. "That's where your father and I stayed the first night we came to England." Newly arrived from Ireland and three months pregnant with me. "I had no idea it was still standing. It was so splendid then. What's it like now?"

"Shades of splendor," I say.

"What on earth are you doing in Liverpool in any case?"

"Finding out about dry rot."

*   *   *

"HE'S a good lad, is our Ken," said Dave, Ken's drinking mate, clutching his seventh pint of the night. "Mad as a hatter, mind you, but a good lad."

Ken just grinned and handed me his pint to hold as someone squeezed past him out the back door of The Crack.

"The Crack?" I'd said as we walked over there. "You're kidding!" But this was a different kind of crack. The cocaine derivative hadn't made it to Liverpool yet; the lads here were into heroin.

"It's the Irish kind of crack," Ken explained. "Like when you go down the pub for a good time with the lads over a pint of Guinness—that's good crack."

I smiled in relief. Cultures crossed once again, that's all. But it felt strange to need an interpreter in your own country.

The sign outside said Ye Olde Crack, and the place looked old enough for that sign not to be an affectation. It was a tiny little pub in an alley. No way you'd get there unless you knew about it. We'd done the tour of Liverpool's most famous pubs that night—the grand old Edwardian and Victorian saloons built by out-of-work shipbuilders and art-college teachers together. Landlocked versions of the ornate luxury steamships of the great transatlantic lines, they were the survivors of the gin-palace days, with stained-glass cupolas, intricate mahogany paneling and bars, beveled ornamental glass, brass detailing, and from the ceilings, massive caryatids looking down on it all. We'd been to The Vines with its mahogany grillwork, the Philharmonic with its splendid wrought-iron gates—female beauties and mythic beasts and flowers woven together in voluptuous baroque disarray—and Peter Kavanagh's, with its risqué oil paintings over the walls, payment in kind for the artist's booze. They were all part of Liverpool lore, and the Beatles, so the lore went, had drunk in all of them.

Outside the Philly, a trio of teenage girls wove unsteadily

down the hill, singing aloud into the night, "Love, love me do, You know I love you . . ."

I hadn't heard that song in years. The girls were born long after it was written. "The mythology is that strong?" I asked Ken.

He nodded. "That's the only mythology Liverpool's got left."

So at the end of an evening of stained glass and mahogany and Beatlephilia, we made for The Crack. Nobody knows if the Beatles drank here, and nobody really cares. They probably did, but so what? Under the low pressed-tin ceilings in the series of tiny rooms, Ken and his friends meet regularly to drink, to chat, to watch football on the television, to play cribbage—to find good crack.

Like Ken, everyone here has that gaunt Merseyside look. Ken has it even though he wasn't born here. Maybe it comes with the wind, the weather, the grayness, the grinding poverty. Ken's parents were born here but went south, precursors of a later mass movement. Born and bred in Cambridge, he never felt quite right, his accent still shadowed with the blunter, warmer vowels of the north. Each summer vacation, his parents would bring him back to Liverpool to see family. "I fell in love with the place like a child falls in love with anywhere he goes on holiday. Of course I was coming back here."

"Mad as a hatter, mind you," said Dave, wondering why anyone would actually choose to live in Liverpool nowadays, as Ken had done, yet grateful that he had.

A football game was playing on the tiny television set high above the bar, and everyone kept one eye on the game as we talked. Liverpool wasn't doing so well that year. "Hasn't been the same since Heysel," someone said.

That was something I'd been wanting to ask about—the riot of Liverpool supporters at a European Cup final in Belgium's Heysel Stadium in 1985, where a retaining wall collapsed causing many deaths and injuries. I'd been holding back, wary of raising a touchy point in a lion's den, but now that someone else had brought it up, I waded on in.

The lions were not as fierce as I'd expected. They were wounded. Ken and Dave and the others seemed more anguished than angry as they explained it to me. It wasn't the Liverpool supporters who started it, they said. It was the Italian supporters of Juventus, the opposing team. Liverpool had been victimized. They were just local lads over in Europe for a good time, to cheer on their team and have a couple of drinks and show the local colors. No harm in that. It was just that by then everyone was picking on English football fans in Europe. If the Italians hadn't started throwing beer on the Liverpool fans, nothing would have happened at all. Most people were hurt because of the panic, not because of what Liverpool fans did or didn't do. It wasn't fair to blame Liverpool.

But they argued with a muted tone of resignation, as though they only half expected to convince me. As though they were resigned to life being unfair to this city. By mutual consent, we didn't dwell on the issue too long. It didn't make for good crack.

I thought I saw my poet friend of old in the press of people, and had to remind myself that he lives in London now, and even there only half of the time. He escapes to southern Spain to write in warmth the rest of the year. I'd looked him up in London before coming to Liverpool. "If I could afford it," he'd said, "I'd get out of England for good."

"Wouldn't you ever go back to Liverpool?" I'd asked.

He shook his head slowly. "I love that city," he said. "But it's desperate, and I've had enough of desperation."

THE next day, I went to revisit the magnificent Victorian palm house in the middle of Sefton Park. It was still there: three-tiered, hexagonal, the palms standing tall inside it. So tall, in fact, that the biggest had broken through some of the panes at the topmost cupola, and poked out, waving in the wind. All the gates were double-padlocked. The palm house was never open now.

I walked around it, shoes squelching in the muddy grass, and counted broken panes. I'd reached fifteen when I nearly bumped into an old man walking his old dog. We stood and stared up at it together.

"They'll be selling this next," he said bitterly. "You got a thousand quid? You can have it, and good luck to you."

I watched him trying to stomp off towards the woods, impelled by pride but slowed down by age and bad legs.

I walked back through the narrow streets between Liverpool 8 and the city center, beneath Hope Street, where addicts picked up clean needles in a new clinic and a few, just a few, found enough courage in the name of the street to stop. Through Pilgrim Street, Mount Pleasant Street, Knight Street, and into the warren of old cobbled alleys lined with brick and wooden warehouses and small artisans' shops. This was once the city's market center; now it's the center for car repairs. Here and there, between the banging and the clanging of dents being straightened and rust being painted over, a small house had been renovated, its wood gleaming new, polished, its eaves pointed and sharp, its grillwork door freshly enameled.

The area is ripe for gentrification. Any New Yorker can see that. The combination of picturesque, old, and rundown in close proximity to the city center is a developer's dream.

"Don't give up, Ken," I said, over a lunchtime beer. "It's going to happen here too."

And he gave me that odd, lopsided grin of his and shook his head. "Oh no, lass, not here. There's no gentry to do it here. They've all moved away long ago."

You can pick up an old house for anywhere from five hundred to five thousand pounds, he said. My New York heart leaped at the idea—a steal! Except that it would cost another fifty to a hundred thousand to make it livable, to root out the dry rot, reline the gutters, treat the walls, put in new beams, a new roof, new floors, new plumbing. And nobody has that kind of money anymore in Liverpool.

In the Albert Dock, the largest grade-one historic renovation in the whole of England with a spectacular view up and down the wide, windy expanse of the Mersey, luxury apartments sell for a mere forty thousand pounds, and even they are going begging.

"Who wants to live in a museum?" said Ken. "That's the last straw, isn't it? It's insulting. All they can think of to do with Liverpool now is make it into a museum."

IT'S easy to feel partisan about a city like Liverpool. It arouses a fierce, protective, quite irrational fondness. The bleakness, the weather, the wind all conspire against that, unsuccessfully. The fondness becomes all the stronger for the struggle. You appreciate its beauty the more for having to look hard for it. And you take its vulnerability more to heart.

How not love a city whose residents are called Liverpudlians? They took the "pool" out of the name and in laughing defiance replaced it with a puddle. How not love a city once known by sailors the world over for its two huge Liver birds, a name pronounced "lye-ver," not "liver." These verdigris-covered creatures spread their wings atop the clock towers of the Liver building, beside the grand old Cunard and Harbour Board buildings on the waterfront. The birds are touchingly ungainly. Where you expect to see grandeur, you see a kind of adult ugly duckling.

In fact, there is no such thing as a Liver bird. It's a Liverpudlian in-joke. Others put eagles atop their public buildings. Liverpool put cormorants.

For centuries, these cormorants presided over the biggest and busiest port in Europe. "In magnitude, cost and durability, the docks of Liverpool surpass all others in the world," wrote Herman Melville in the early nineteenth century. "For miles you may walk along the riverside passing dock after dock like a chain of immense fortresses. Each Liverpool dock is a walled town full of life and commotion."

No mere mooring places, these, but huge brick and stone edifices built around deep docks, with a narrow entrance leading in from the river, controlled by locks. Salt, iron, coal, and cloth went out of Liverpool; wool, flax, tobacco, and sugar came in. And until 1807, when slavery was banned in the British Empire, Liverpool was one of the three corners of the slave triangle. Ships left for the west coast of Africa loaded with manufactured goods, which they exchanged for slaves; they shipped the slaves transatlantic to America, exchanged them for tobacco and sugar, and came on back to Liverpool. The city was rich. Merchants and shipbuilders made fortunes. The Georgian terraces in Liverpool 8 were full of consulates and rich men's mansions, sitting atop the hill where their owners could look down on the docks and survey their empires. When steamships came in the 1840s, the port became busier still, the main terminal for the massive Cunard and White Star ocean liners. Airplanes, containerization, and the end of Empire were still far away.

Most of the docks are gone now. Some are just closed up, empty and derelict; others have been destroyed. A few still work, further down towards the mouth of the Mersey, but even they are struggling. This is no place for those who love docks. Except for museum-goers.

The Albert Dock was one of the finest. A gigantic square complex, almost a mile's walk around its walls, it has been renovated in the Faneuil Hall–South Street Seaport tradition. Gentrified, that is. Five stories tall, it has vaulted brick arches spanning to cast-iron beams and columns. Where Melville saw the commotion of a port at the height of its business, today you can stroll the ground floor buying knick-knacks from the usual assortment of boutiques and souvenir shops. Or you can visit the Maritime Museum. Or stand dumbfounded, as I did one morning, staring at the brass sign that announced The Museum of Emigration—in the basement.

A museum tailor-made, it seemed, for me.

I don't know of any other city that celebrates its history as a port of exit. New York, Sydney, Cape Town, Haifa—these pride themselves on having been ports of entry. There is something very sad, and very touching, when a city celebrates the opposite. When it celebrates the fact that it was the lodestone for those so poor that all they owned was what they traveled with, those whose hopes for a different future were focused far away, across the Atlantic.

Millions of them passed through Liverpool. Nearly ten million, to be exact. Millions forced out by poverty, as with the Irish, or by prejudice, as with the Jews.

And to me, the daughter of Irish Jews on the threshold of being accepted into America, it seemed as though here, in the basement, was where I belonged.

The ten million left between 1830 and 1930, mainly for the United States, but also for Canada and Australia. Most came from Britain and Ireland, but there were many other Europeans too— people from Germany, Russia, Scandinavia, who'd traveled by boat to Hull, on the west coast, crossed northern England by train, then embarked again at Liverpool.

I wandered around, pressing all the buttons on all the displays like a ten-year-old, pressing them just for the pleasure of watching emigration routes light up, different colors for different routes and different nationalities. The idea was for Americans to trace their heritage, but I knew I wouldn't find mine here. My great-grandparents had booked passage from Latvia to New York, and been unceremoniously turfed off the boat at Bantry, on the south coast of Ireland, when the captain announced he went thus far, and no farther. They didn't even know that Liverpool was the place they needed. Two generations later, my parents would spend a night in Liverpool, their first night as immigrants to England from Ireland. Another generation, and I was finally carrying out my great-grandparents' dream.

I played computer games with myself, choosing old sailing-ship routes, encountering storms at sea, mutinies, outbreaks of epidemic disease on board. My ships got held up again and again. It seemed I'd never make it to America. I picked up a telephone and heard a nineteenth-century girl reading from her diary, written in a bedbug-ridden rooming house as she and her family waited for passage that would never come. They'd been gypped of all their belongings right after arriving in Liverpool; they could never afford the passage now. They'd become Liverpudlians. I flicked a switch on a video display and watched the jerky speeded-up movement of immigrants boarding steerage on an ocean steamer in 1923. So much hope bound up in the bundles over their shoulders, in the gaunt, hungry faces, the huge, dark eyes—faces and bundles that would soon fill the tenements of the Lower East Side of New York, where I now lived in my renovated condominium apartment in what had once been an arts settlement house. For all I knew, some of those people I was watching on the screen had studied English in my living room, tongues twisting with exhaustion after sixteen-hour sweatshop stints, determined that come what may, America would do for their children and grandchildren what it was too late to do for them.

There were Jewish faces on that screen—the lucky ones, the prescient ones, getting out in time. Before the United States tightened its immigration laws. Before it closed the doors to refugees from Hitler's Europe. Before escape was no longer possible.

I wiped tears from my cheeks, not quite sure how they'd gotten there. A group of chattering school kids saw, and a hush came over them as they passed by. Their giggles and chatter picked up again behind me. I sat down on a small bench and searched in my purse for a Kleenex, confused by my own emotion. And shamed.

Boat people—always boats full of desperate people. There are millions of third-world would-be immigrants today, Asians and Central Americans, boat people and refugees. People who still, today, make those sacrifices and hazard those risks to travel to a foreign shore, a foreign culture, a foreign language, in the stubborn, defiant determination that their children will have it better than they. The faces had changed, but the story hadn't. And suddenly my own story, my own year-long tussle with the bureaucracy of the Immigration and Naturalization Service, no matter how frustratingly arcane and complicated it had seemed to me, was paltry and easy by comparison. My immigration to the States was one of choice; theirs was one of desperate need. The difference is crucial, and humbling.

I joined the school kids, tagging along behind them as costumed actors guided us through a reconstruction of the Liverpool emigrant experience, mid-nineteenth century. There was the confusion and commotion on the quays. The thieves and pickpockets and runners, offering to look after our belongings and then disappearing with them. The cramped creaking quarters of the ship, with makeshift wooden bunks leaving no room to move. The stench of vomit and sweat, excrement and urine, stale food and stale air. The sounds—voices, moans of illness and seasickness, arguments, crying children, the babble of hope and helplessness and frustration.

Timber and cotton had come over to Liverpool in the holds of such ships; passengers made a good return cargo. Passage cost four pounds—as much as it costs now to stand in the terraces for a soccer game. A month's wages then, if you had a job. And the conditions so bad, with so many dying en route, that in 1852 they had to pass a Passenger Act, laying down minimal standards.

The trip to America took three weeks. Later, when the steamships came, it would take ten days. Seven of the ten million went to the States. To Ellis Island. And as we emerged from the reconstruction, we walked into an exhibit of New York harbor, surrounded by portraits of famous immigrants who'd come through Liverpool: Sam Goldwyn, JFK's great-grandfather, Woodrow Wilson's mother, Butch Cassidy's father.

The school kids enjoyed it. It was fun to feel what it was like in the hold of an old sailing ship. But I wondered what they'd learn from all this. For most it would be just another school outing, one more day's relief from the penance of the school desk and tests and homework. A diversion, no more. For one or two it might even be what it was intended to be—a lesson in Liverpool's history. But for some, I felt sure, an unintended lesson would be learned—a lesson of yearning, of ambition and escape. For the main message of Liverpool's Museum of Emigration was writ large in invisible letters you'd have to be blind not to see:

"Go west, young man." Go to America.

MASQUERADE

I had gone to America. And the main reason I was back in England now was to get my American immigration papers. After a year-long bureaucratic odyssey, the elusive quarry was in sight. It would take the form of the Green Card, the official American immigrant visa.

The Green Card is the biggest and most difficult hurdle on the road to becoming an American. Objectively speaking, it's a small piece of plastic the size of a charge card that declares its owner a permanent resident of the United States. But once you begin the quest for one, objectivity becomes cruelly irrelevant, and the Green Card achieves mythic proportions.

The Green Card: three magic words all but unknown to most Americans, but for which people are ready to swear, lie, pay their life's savings, give an arm or an eye or a leg, and even—as some have—to risk death.

It's the dream of the Third World, of peasants in Central America, of field laborers in Asia, of intellectuals in Lagos and doctors in Ireland, of engineers in Egypt, scientists in England and artists in Czechoslovakia.

It's a symbol, a promise, a kind of Holy Grail that haunts the dreams and the waking lives of restless people the world over.

It's the fantasy of freedom, the dream of riches, the magic "open sesame" that is the key to America.

It's the pride of every immigrant, the impossible ambition of every peasant, the gateway to the yellow brick road.

The Green Card: the first three words of an unwritten ode to opportunity. Or a love song to America.

In fact, I had been quite happy without one. I'd been living in the States for seven years on a temporary working visa, renewable by the year. Each year, another page of my British passport was taken up by the big blue stamp, the largest and most official looking of any visa I'd ever received. I knew how difficult it was to get a Green Card; smugly, I thought I didn't need one. Until, that is, they changed the rules.

Henceforth, temporary working visas could only be held for a maximum of six years. I was over seven. I had no choice. Everything temporary comes to an end; it was time for a permanent commitment.

So over the past year, I had accumulated a three-inch-thick file with the Immigration and Naturalization Service, had done yeoman service in the ranks of battle with three government departments—Labor, State, and Justice, each of which had to approve my application—and had marveled at modern bureaucracy's ability to out-Kafka Kafka.

Now I was near the end of my Green Card odyssey. I could almost feel it in my hand. All that remained was to present myself at the American Embassy in London at ten in the morning on July 13, undergo some medical tests, submit myself to a formal interview, cross my fingers, and pray.

In fact I could have completed the whole process in the United States, but I wanted to mark this transition with something more than stamps and signatures on a piece of paper. I felt as though I were getting married after years of living with someone; the objective facts of my life would remain unchanged, yet the existence of a marriage contract would subtly change them. Immigration, like marriage, seemed to demand deliberate thought and recognition. The formal change in country of residence was surely a good time for a psychic polling, some form of coming to terms with where I had come from, and what I had left behind. It was no longer enough to say I had left England; I needed a more definite acknowledgement of why I had left. And I needed to know to what degree I was still English—in fact, to what degree I had ever really been English.

I had decided to come to England three months earlier than I needed to. That would give me time to explore the country I'd once thought was mine. I'd find old friends and old familiar places, and flesh out the ghosts of my past. I'd wander through the class system, with access to both upper and lower classes assured by virtue of my acquired foreignness. I'd see what I might have been, what I'd escaped, and what had come into being since I'd left.

I knew this was strange work to be doing in a native country. Like everyone, I assumed that if you grew up in a place, you knew it. But this doesn't necessarily apply to England. And despite the fact that I'd been born there, grew up there, and was clearly identifiable as English everywhere in the world except in England itself, the country was still an enigma to me.

I'd been English for the first twenty years of my life—or at least I'd tried to be. Those twenty years had formed and shaped me, even though all that time I'd felt stifled, constricted into a way of life, behavior and manners that was not mine, and that would not allow me to find out what was mine. I'd had to leave in order to discover that.

And now another twenty years had gone by. I'd spent thirteen of those years in the Middle East, and then moved to the States. I had enough perspective by now, I thought. England was my childhood, but the impassioned drama of the Middle East had changed me, as had the energy and vitality of New York life. I still had my English passport, but my own Englishness seemed keener away from England than in it. It was only in England that I realized how far I had traveled.

When I left in 1966 I had no idea I was leaving for good. Sometimes the unconscious is wiser than the conscious. I was as shy and repressed as any upper-middle-class young English lady should be. Israel was like shock therapy. It was as though someone had suddenly raised the ante—doubled and tripled it. The base values of well-bred English social communication—repression, inhibition, indirection—were wonderfully irrelevant. Instead of the cold, damp blanket of Englishness, there was noise and rudeness, vibrancy and color, drama and warmth and passion.

I was utterly seduced. I'd never realized life could be so interesting. And though I was incapable of stating it at the time, I knew then I could never go back to live in England.

OTHER cultures make you see your own in a way you never could before. They distance you from it emotionally. When an old friend, back in England after years in Italy, discussed this with me, both he and I automatically referred to the English as "they."

"I never know what English people are thinking," he said.

"Do they know what each other is thinking?" I asked.

"There are subtle signs," he replied. "It's like cracking a code."

The trouble is that nobody seems to have the key to that code.

It's as though the code has become so entrenched that it has usurped the place of the meaning it was supposed to mask. It has worked its way deep into the language, where the most common form of public pronouncement is the impersonal "one," and where prevarication is the norm.

"One does tend to wonder, doesn't one?"

"One can't help thinking that perhaps . . ."

"One wouldn't be terribly keen on that sort of thing around here, would one?"

The code becomes more complex when it includes those careful, elegant little phrases that take the punch out of a statement when it's written on the page, yet somehow add to it when spoken with the right insinuating intonation.

"Under certain circumstances, of course . . ."

"Now you come to mention it . . ."

Or the infamous, completely disarming power of a subtly intoned "Do you really think so?" or simply, "Oh really?"

Such phrases imply a deeper knowledge. In fact, more often than not, they mask ignorance. But American Anglophiles adore them, mistaking them for sophistication. In the same way, they admire the British facility with complex sentences, as though the ornate were by definition more sophisticated than the spare. Certainly, given the right circumstances and, so to speak, the will to do so, one can construct what might be called a reasonably complex sentence—even, dare one say, an extremely complex one— with all the qualifying clauses in the right places, and sometimes the wrong ones, but in the long run, or so it seems at this particular juncture in time, one can also qualify any meaning at all to the point where it no longer exists, which is to say that one can hedge and trim, parry and prevaricate, so that by the end of the sentence the reader may be left floored, stunned even, by the elegance of its structure, and only later get round to wondering what exactly had been said. Or not said.

Qualify, qualify. Avoid direct statement. Elude the dangers of the first person singular. Stick to the good old "one"—the generic impersonal English self. Avoid the effrontery, the egotism, the vulgar assertiveness of the first person singular. Who do you think you are, anyway?

Language reflects thought. In Western civilization, it's the framework of thought. This "one" depersonalizes the individual. It establishes a distance between the individual and the world.

"One doesn't say such things," you are told. But what happens if you just did? Are you then not a "one"? Are you expelled from the society of "ones"?

It's a slippery business, this "one." It represents a consensus, something that everyone knows, which makes it basically unchallengeable except by the weak response of an insinuating "doesn't one?" It's a final authority, like God. And though one doesn't wish to appear blasphemous, it does make one wonder, doesn't it?

ENGLISH politeness: At a Chinese restaurant in Manhattan—small tables, closely packed—an Englishwoman at the table behind me rises to go, and has to lift my coat to reach hers.

"I'm so sorry," she says to me. "Oh dear, I'm really so sorry."

She apologizes profusely, as though I were about to snap her head off for daring to disturb my coat's repose. She pats my coat back into place, gives me a strained smile, and apologizes yet again.

I smile back, my smile forced by my embarrassment at her embarrassment. "That's quite all right," I say. "No, really . . ." We play the English game.

"It's hard being English," I say to my dinner partner once she's gone. "It means you have to apologize all the time."

I say it sympathetically. I remember what it was like. There was always that fear—yes, fear—of overstepping some undefined boundary. The phrases float back across time: "Keep your place." "It's not done." "Don't make a display of yourself." And the demeaning "Who do you think you are, anyway?" Phrases designed to cut down any uppity assertion of self.

"It's that wonderful English politeness," say American Anglophiles. "The English are so considerate."

But they're not. The politeness is less consideration of others than sheer embarrassment at the very fact of being.

To be English is to exist in a constant state of embarrassment. Objectively speaking, surely nobody could possibly have that much to be embarrassed about. But the forms of English communication and culture are designed to heighten self-consciousness, and to reinforce a sense of "one's" place in the social hierarchy.

Stepping out of bounds, admired as audacity in American society, is seen in England as the most severe of social sins.

To be English is thus to be in an uncomfortable position in the world. You can never be sure if you are doing anything right. It is to suffer from a surfeit of self-consciousness, and a continuing uncertainty about both yourself and others. What are they thinking? What did you just say? Are you okay? Are they okay? The American bestseller *I'm O.K., You're O.K.* seemed astonishingly crude to the English, who are always searching for but never acknowledge the social signals to assure them that they are okay. Crude, and yet at the same time enviable in its naive assurance.

Take the prototypical young Englishman as limned by William Boyd, one of England's rising young novelists who is fascinated by America and writes the English stereotype of Americans—mad cowboy millionaires, voracious nymphomaniacs, gun-toting rednecks, that sort of thing. Here is the hero of *Stars and Bars,* the innocent, rather upper-class young Englishman abroad, written with tongue only half in cheek.

"He was (he categorized himself with no trace of self-pity) a shy man. Not chronically shy—he didn't stammer or spit or flinch or sweat in the manner of the worst afflicted—no, he was shy in the way most of his countrymen were shy. His flaw was a congenital one: latent, deep, ever present. It was like having a birthmark or a dormant illness, a racial configuration. . . .

"True, his education and his upbringing provided him with a reasonably efficient kit of tools and methods to overcome his disability. Observe him nattering at a cocktail party; see him engage his dull partner at a dinner table with conversation and one would never guess the nature of his disease. But it was there, and beneath this sociocultural veneer he suffered from all the siblings of shyness too: the feeble air of confidence, the formulaic self-possession, a conditioned wariness of emotional display, a distrust of spontaneity, a dread fear of attracting attention, an almost irrepressible urge to conform."

Pity the poor Englishman, bound into self-consciousness, restricted by the mask of manners built into English upper- and middle-class life. Emotional display is vulgar, lower-class, which is perhaps why lower-class life seems so warm, direct, and refreshing by comparison—and why the longest running soaps in England, such as "Coronation Street" and "EastEnders," are of lower-class life.

England is still a class-ridden society, with people identifiable by class the moment they open their mouths. But the last thirty years or so have seen a subtle change in class status as younger members of the middle and upper classes detected a spontaneity in lower-class life entirely missing in their own. Since the emergence of the Beatles made England a focal point for rock music, upper-class young Britons have affected lower-class accents in an odd effort to show themselves à la mode. It's rather like white Americans affecting black jive talk—terribly hip, and just as condescending. But there's also a certain bathos to it: It's an effort to enter into a world that seems much looser and happier, despite the lack of status and money, than their own. In their own ham-fisted way, they are searching for a way out of the mask of manners.

That mask clamps down on expression of feeling. If it gives way, that's shameful, rather like a tattered slip showing beneath the hem of a skirt. The mask is part of the cult of privacy—the maintaining of a clear barrier between public and private lives and selves, between the clean, pressed skirt and the grubby slip.

Any breakdown in this mask is like the lid coming off a pressure cooker: eruption. Inevitably, breakdowns happen in the lower class, where the pent-up rage shared by the middle and upper classes is closer to the surface. Whether in football hooliganism or in racist attacks on Asian immigrants, the horror is that of so much tightly repressed emotion suddenly finding release. Violence is the underside of manners, the tragic mask behind the wryly comic one.

In a country where the barrier between public and private is so strong it seems to penetrate even to the innermost self, such violent eruptions are probably inevitable. What other release is there? Psychotherapy is still seen as a shameful matter, too much a threat to that inner privacy by which the English remain unknown even to themselves. The American love affair with self-exploration is seen as vulgar, almost childish. Where Americans verbalize, the English can only internalize.

The oblique subtlety of a Harold Pinter play, where as much is said in the silences as in speech, is quintessentially English. Words become barriers instead of bridges. The play of words revolves around irony, shame, bewilderment, a cutting cruelty that depends on the secondary modes of expression and emotion—nothing so vulgar as the primary emotions of love, hate, anger.

The roisterous, boisterous feel of contemporary American theater is an ocean apart. More than an ocean—another world, another culture. A vast volume of words floods the stage in a Sam Shepard or David Mamet play; words fly, speed, pile up on each other, pour out in a virtuoso display of volubility. Characters hurl them at each other, at the world, at the universe, as though by just speaking they could overcome their limitations, become as big as they dream of being. Where the English use words as a means of control, weighing them carefully, parting with them sparingly, Americans use them in aggressive assertion of their place in the world.

Language reflects culture. Some say it *is* culture. The vitality of American culture comes rollicking through the language, and anyone in England with a taste for life can only look on in envy.

America seems to have the energy England lacks, the outspokenness and the vitality. Which is why more and more of the English are looking west—and going west. What was once considered vulgar has become exciting. It's as though the English are tired of being English. It's too much like hard work. There have to be more enjoyable ways to live.

So on either side of the Atlantic, cultures envy each other.

English Americaphiles look across the Atlantic and see life writ large, with all its virtues and all its faults. American Anglophiles look across the same ocean and see a stereotype of sophistication, a myth of Empire. They ignore the vicious racism, the repressiveness of the class system, the dulled isolationism within which most English people live their lives. They admire the form, and ignore the content. Perhaps you have to be English to know how little meaning there is in form, how stifling it can be, and how tempting the American vision by contrast.

If it weren't for Green Card restrictions, there would be a full-scale flood of British immigrants seeking a new life in America—twentieth-century counterparts of the original Pilgrims. Even with the restrictions, there are more English immigrants to the United States than from all other European countries combined.

Now I was about to become one of them. Once that would have been considered highly peculiar in England, but with each visit back over the past few years, I had found myself more and more an object of envy. I was one of the ones who had made it out, an adventurer who had found shelter on a foreign shore and had come back with exotic tales of palm trees and native beauties, strange customs and loose, uninhibited ways. And like Victorians wondering about the sanity of some of their returned explorers, some English people now looked at me and wondered if I hadn't "gone native," succumbed to the enticements of that foreign land and lost my sense of Englishness.

What they didn't realize is that, like many of those Victorian adventurers, this had been my purpose all along.

SHOCKING LIME

THE little girl plopped down beside me on the couch. Its flowery cotton print was the kind currently known in the States as English style. She folded her hands in her lap and stared up at me wide-eyed, as though waiting for the curtain to lift on a theater performance.

She was dressed in her Sunday best: a pretty velvet frock with lace trimming, white socks and black patent shoes, and a big bow at the back of her head. I was dressed casually. Too casually. She examined every detail of my clothing as though she'd never seen anything quite like this before. I was a whole new phenomenon to be absorbed.

I wished I'd worn something better than jeans; I wished I'd never brought my sneakers to England; I wished I had something more subtle than the collarless houndstooth jacket, which may have seemed stylish in Manhattan's East Village but here in suburban Kent was . . . well, loud.

I wished, in fact, that I'd never traced her mother, my old school friend Charlotte, and called her. She'd stammered and hesitated on the phone, flustered by this sudden call from the past. "Oh well, oh goodness gracious, well I never . . ." But then what do you say when someone suddenly calls and announces that she's your best friend from twenty-five years ago? Especially when this someone sounds unmistakably foreign on the phone. American, in fact.

You ask them for Sunday tea, which is exactly what Charlotte did. Except that I'd been so long out of England that I misread the invitation as a casual "come over for some tea on Sunday." I forgot that "Sunday tea" is another thing altogether—an institution, in fact—which is how come I was so inappropriately dressed.

It was a cold June day, overcast with rain threatening. As I'd set out from London to drive down to Kent, I'd begun to wonder if this was such a great idea. It could have been considered normal enough: a sudden desire to see an old school friend again, a journalist's ability to trace her whereabouts, and presto—I was on my way for tea. Simple curiosity, I thought, as I meandered along in the slow lane, letting the Sunday traffic overtake me. But I knew that wasn't it. I was looking for something, and I wasn't sure what. Looking for what I might have been, perhaps, if I'd stayed in England. Except I already knew.

There was no doubt at all in my mind that if I'd never left England, I would have gone the way that was laid out for me. There would have been no opportunity to move into anything else. I'd be whatever level of academic was appropriate for my age and sex, teaching psychology in one of the redbrick universities, maybe one of the new ones set up in the sixties. The closed-track system of English education and opportunity would have dictated that.

So just what was it I expected from this sudden visit? A mirror of my former self? A picture of a road not traveled? I wasn't sure, and as I drove deeper into the country, misgiving began to nag at me.

We were eight years old when we first became friends. Both of us thin and wiry, both with unruly hair that resisted the braids it had been forced into, I with a long sallow face, she with a round pale face with bright red cheeks, a high voice, and a continual appetite for mischief gleaming in her eyes. It was that mischief that brought us together—a shared boredom, a desire to make school more lively, to test the limits. She was less shy than I, more adventurous. I'd have to leave England to discover the extent of my own adventurousness. And she? What had happened to hers?

As I rolled by the polite green of the Kent countryside, I remembered the two of us hatching plans; daring each other into flipping an ink pellet, tripping a prefect on the hockey field, playing faint in class. We vied for who could get the most black stars in deportment. We were both bright, with an array of gold stars for studies, so the long line of black stars next to our names on the classroom board became a challenge, a counterbalance, a reassurance that we were just two of the girls, racing and sliding along the highly polished school corridors, screaming and giggling.

In hockey, she played center forward, I center half, and we were invincible on the field. The same in netball: I set up the scoring position, she dropped the ball in the net. We had the track and field covered, with her winning the long jump, high jump, and javelin, and I the sprinting and hurdles. We were the perfect pair. In an old school photograph I found several years ago in my parents' house, we stand side by side, knobbly kneed in our gym slips, grinning maniacally into the camera. We must have been about eleven then. Four years later we'd drift apart, she to the sciences, I to the humanities, and by the time we left school we hardly saw each other. I couldn't even remember saying goodbye.

Now I turned off the motorway, followed the road into a small town, got lost in the one-way system, and finally found the house in a small cul-de-sac just outside town. Chestnut trees shaded the road. About a half-dozen houses were set back on either side, each one different, each one perfectly maintained. It was a road for kids to tricycle up and down, for dogs to roam and race after balls and frisbees, for homecoming parents to pat their own and neighbor's children on the head as they got out of their cars at the end of a long day's work. But there were no kids to be seen. Or dogs. The road was absolutely quiet.

The front garden was in a state of perfection. Not a petal, not a leaf, not a single blade of grass was out of place. I rang the doorbell—a muffled tinkle somewhere inside the house—and waited awkwardly.

Charlotte's husband answered the door, hesitated a moment as though he wasn't sure what to do with my outstretched hand, then shook it and ushered me into the living room. It was full of fake suede plush and patterned wallpaper and knick-knacks in glass showcases. I felt conspicuously out of place.

French windows opened onto a small patio and a back garden as immaculate as one in a house-and-garden magazine— impeccably shaped trees, creepers lying in perfect symmetry over a trellis, borders carefully graded for the height and colors of the flowers, everything pruned, nipped, sheared, edged, mowed and trimmed, just so.

I turned and saw a matronly woman in a silky summer dress with a big floral pattern, the kind of dress women wore to garden parties at Buckingham Palace. She had a halo of stiff blond hair, neatly curled and waved à la Margaret Thatcher, and stood in the doorway with her hands clasped tightly in front of her.

We looked, and before we had time to cover it up, what we saw in each other's eyes was horror. I saw the stereotype of the suburban housewife; she saw an outlandishly dressed foreigner.

"Well," said Charlotte. She sat down stiffly in an easy chair, looking at me as though I might leap on her and force more words out of her. "Well." A single word dropped into the void.

A long silence, and then I started babbling.

God help me but I couldn't stop. I was so embarrassed, and Charlotte was so embarrassed, and the husband was so embarrassed that he had disappeared. I didn't know what else to do. I talked fast, telling tales of a different world, my American world, stories that might amuse and delight over a New York dinner table, but that here in Kent on a Sunday afternoon, sounded foreign even to my ears. And the more I babbled, the stronger my American accent became, as though to reinforce my own sense of difference.

Finally I wound down. There was another long silence.

"We were in America, last year," she said. "We went to Tampa, in Florida."

I leaned forward to hear more. There was no more.

"Why I was just there this spring," I said. "I was on assignment, covering spring training with the Mets." And off I went again, chattering on about my American obsession—baseball, for God's sake, in Kent!—until to my horror I was describing what it was like to sit on the locker-room steps chewing tobacco:

"It's like a direct injection of nicotine, straight into your veins."

Oh God, stop me, please—just stop me.

"We went to Disney World," said Charlotte.

That stopped me. Dead in my tracks.

"We liked it," she said. "It was very interesting."

I sat on the edge of the couch waiting for more, but that was it.

I tried "whatever-happened-to-so-and-so," but Charlotte had lost touch with most of the others in our school class, and the ones she remembered, I couldn't remember at all. I asked what work she did, but she hadn't held a job in years and seemed to think it quite amazing that she'd ever set foot in a laboratory, as though that were some other life, not hers.

"Would you like some coffee?" she said abruptly.

I hardly ever drink coffee.

"I'd love some," I said with relief. "Here, let me help you make it."

"Oh no, please don't." And she was out of the room before I could say any more.

I was left with Charlotte's daughter, who was clearly fascinated. She was eight years old, and she stared at me with the frankness of an eight-year-old anywhere in the world. And hadn't I stared that way once myself, long ago?

How old was I that summer day when Aunt Chuck came to

visit? Was I the same age? About eight? I must have been nearly that. I remember the awnings were down over the huge flagstone terrace of our house and all the French windows were open; from the orchard there came a faint scent of ripeness on the breeze. They were blue, fringed awnings, shading the windows and part of the long terrace above the steps that led down to the lawn. On summer Sunday afternoons, my mother would bring out glasses of lemonade on a big straw tray while my father finished mowing the lawn, my brother and I scampering to help empty the bin of the lawn mower, heaving loads of fragrant new-mown grass over to the compost heap. I'd run ahead of the voracious blades of the mower, picking daisies and making daisy-chains, yards of them at a time, which then wilted on the terrace as I tired of the game and went on to something else.

This particular Sunday—a sunny one, as all the best childhood days seem to be, even in England—we'd finished mowing the lawn and turned on the sprinklers. I was lying beneath the spray, watching the rainbow in the drops of water arching over me, when Aunt Chuck arrived.

I'd never even heard of her until that day. She was my father's aunt, my great-aunt, and she lived in America. Chuck— the first American name I'd ever heard. I rolled it around my mouth like a new taste, surprised at the abrupt friendliness of it. Had she always been Chuck, growing up in Bantry, Ireland, or was that the name she'd adopted when she got off the boat on the other side of the Atlantic? I didn't know enough then to ask. At that age, you accept the givens of the adult world in much the same way that Catholics accept the mysteries.

I heard the commotion of arrival—the dog barking, my mother's voice raised in effusive welcome, my brother being told to say hello. And then, under the arc of the sprinkler's rainbow, I saw her step out onto the terrace in the brightest green dress I'd ever seen—a loud and vulgar and joyful green, a green that would glow in the dark, a green to make you rub your eyes and look again and yet again. A shocking, a wonderfully shocking, bright lime green!

I'd never seen that color before. I had no idea it even existed. I rolled over onto my stomach and lifted my head to see better. The dress was a linen shift, sleeveless and elegant, and she wore it with a carefree casualness that seemed to shout all the way from the terrace: "Come on, look! See what fun life can be!"

Behind me, the Union Jack fluttered from the flagpole at the edge of the lawn. In front of me, her voice came floating over from the terrace, louder than the others, broader, with drawling, open American vowels. They were vowels that spoke of an appetite for things new and wondrous, an appetite for life. Vowels that spoke with exclamation marks! Vowels that rode roughshod over the clipped, closed English vowels my parents had adopted.

I heard my name being called. "Come and say hello to your Aunt Chuck," shouted loud from the terrace. And then, still carrying, though quieter: "I don't know what's got into that girl, she's such a dreamer."

Something in my mother's voice spoke of discomfort, of some unease that had entered an orderly world. Only in England can a voice convey such things so quickly and so subtly. A certain strain to it, perhaps, a particular tension that you have to be English to catch.

I trotted out from under the sprinkler and over the lawn, up the steps to the terrace, ready to have my hair tousled, or a perfumed cheek bend down to be kissed, or a voice pronounce me "a delightful child," or any of the other meaningless compliments to my mother which completely ignored my scraped-kneed gawkishness and assumed a child unable to detect condescension.

Instead of which, Aunt Chuck sat down, looked me straight in the eyes, and said: "So you're a tomboy. That's great!"

"Aren't you going to kiss your Aunt Chuck?" my mother said. Aunt Chuck ignored her. So did I.

"I was one myself once," she said. "Maybe I still am."

I decided right then and there that there was no better color in the world than shocking lime green.

AND now Charlotte's daughter stared at me. That accent! Those stories! Her parents' evident discomfort! It all added up to a world she'd had no idea existed—another, alien world where the rules didn't apply, suddenly appeared here on her living-room couch as though transported by spaceship.

As her mother made coffee, the girl and I began to talk toys. "Do you want to see the ones I've made?" she asked.

"But of course," I said.

She went running out. Charlotte shook her head as she served the coffee and cake. "That girl," she sighed disapprovingly.

The girl came back bearing a shoe box. Together, we moved the coffee cups and plates of cake aside, and then one by one she brought her treasures out of the box.

She'd molded plastilene into miniature riots of color, then baked it hard into tiny cats and diamond-shaped abstracts, pots and dragons, trees and tables, balls and people. We arranged them all on the table, laughing, then rearranged them again and again, making up stories about them as we went along. The coffee spilled into the saucers as we pushed the cups further to one side. Charlotte looked on in silence.

And then I remembered I had a camera in the car. I dashed out to get it, and as I came back in, registered the look of resignation on Charlotte's face.

"But of course," it seemed to say. "Americans are always photographing things. What else could one expect?"

The child beamed as we experimented with angles. We took shots of her toys from the top, from eye level, from beneath. We rearranged them yet again and took more. There was the luxury of taking more than one shot, and the fun of trying out different angles. But more, there was the pride of knowing that your work is good enough to be photographed, and the sheer hubris of insisting that something temporary be immortalized on film.

Yes, I was the American come to visit, and once I recognized that image in the girl's eyes, I lost all my self-consciousness and played it to the hilt. Look, see what fun it can be. Forget the rules, the tidiness, the shoulds and should nots. We can be loud and vulgar, we can immortalize ourselves, we can be noisily proud of what we've done. We can enjoy it!

But what excited the girl, seemed to horrify her mother. I don't know for sure what Charlotte thought of me that day, as we sat through the uncomfortable ritual of high tea, with quiche and salads and breads and cakes served on the prettily laid dining-room table and the girl sent out to draw on the kitchen table since this was for adults. But just as I searched in her for the girl I used to know, she must have done the same with me. Both of us came up blank, and all we had to fall back on was the stilted formality of tea-table conversation.

Perhaps it would have happened that way in any case, no matter if I'd left England or not. Perhaps it was just a matter of personalities, not of experience. But I don't really believe that. The divide between us was too deep and too broad—as broad and as deep as the Atlantic Ocean.

The element of betrayal loomed large. She had become the Englishwoman she was destined to be. I had rejected all that, and gone about the task of creating myself in a different image—an American image, an image remembered from a faraway childhood day.

I doubt if I gave Aunt Chuck much thought once she left later that day. A child's life is too full of events for any particular one to linger long in consciousness. But that doesn't mean I'd forgotten her. Only that she was sitting there, a lime green presence somewhere in my mind, waiting to re-emerge. As she did that cold June Sunday, thirty-odd years and two continents later, in a small Kentish town. And in the wide eyes of my old school friend's daughter I saw my own, staring up at the vision that was Chuck.

Ah Chuck, were you real? Luminous American in the light of a summer's afternoon with a name so unlikely that even now I wonder if I didn't imagine you—didn't *need* to imagine you. Sweet Aunt Chuck in your lime green dress and the fine elegance of little gold sandals, long tanned naked legs and arms, with that gold snake bracelet circling your right wrist. Its tiny emerald eye twinkled in the sunlight so that it seemed to wink at me, as your eyes did. Carelessly extravagant Chuck, so innocently outrageous as the discomfort flashed on my parents' faces: little looks that said "Oh dear, that voice! Couldn't she just talk more quietly? And that color! And no stockings!" The embarrassed looks the English adopted in the fifties when confronted with the openness of an American. The looks that said "How on earth are we going to get through this afternoon?"

And through it all, Chuck, you kept right on talking, impervious, smiling, glinting in the sunlight. I wanted you to talk and talk, and you did, and those long, drawling, open vowels washed over me like the spray from the sprinkler and I saw the rainbows arching in them, unsuspected glimpses of another, hidden world of vivacity and color.

Where did you live, Chuck? What did you do with your life? I never asked. You may have lived in Florida, married for the third time, filled out your days with pinochle and bridge and heartbreak rummy and Hadassah meetings, but if so, that's not my concern. Real life doesn't apply to you, not for me. You were the first intimation of something bigger, some way of life that could be full of appetite and enjoyment, loud laughter and directness and ease.

What year was it then? Fifty-three or fifty-four it must have been, and Queen Elizabeth newly crowned, and the globe still reassuringly covered in various shades of pink—light pink for Commonwealth, dark pink for Empire. Every way you turned the tin globe in its cheap brass clasp, there was pink, and below the big pink of Canada, the wild green space of America. Which even on a tin globe, turned in the sun, could light up luridly in faint imitation of your lime green dress.

You were a revelation of America to me. You were daring, loud, extravagant. You showed me something I didn't even know I hungered for as the sheer vitality of your presence spoke of other worlds out there, where the rules didn't apply. Where you didn't have to be English.

And somewhere inside my timid, quiet, polite English soul, an as yet unacknowledged voice responded in kind, saying, "Yes—this is what I want!"

EXPULSIONS

NOT long after they arrived in England, my parents settled in the southern town of Reading, where I was born. My father had just graduated from the Royal College of Surgeons, Ireland, and like most Irish professionals, then as now, he looked overseas for his future. Many crossed the Atlantic; he was considered one of the lucky ones who only had to go as far as England.

Reading is a comfortable, middle-class town, the kind of town that is famous for small things. Set in the Thames valley halfway between London and Oxford, it was a good place to grow up—and a good place to leave. It has two major claims to fame for anyone of a mildly literary bent. The first is that T. E. Lawrence—Lawrence of Arabia—left the entire manuscript of *Seven Pillars of Wisdom* on a bench in Reading station while the train was stopped between London and Oxford. The manuscript disappeared and he wrote the whole book over again, from scratch. That is, if you like, the prototypical Reading story— the town as transit stop, the incidental location, a footnote to greatness.

Its second claim to literary fame is as a jail town: Oscar Wilde was imprisoned there after he was convicted for homosexuality, and thus graced English literature with *The Ballad of Reading Gaol.* This was never mentioned in the town when I was growing up. It was one of those things that you had to discover by yourself, in the library or the bookstore, wide-eyed at the very idea that anything so interesting, let alone risqué, could possibly have happened in Reading.

But Reading has a third and far older claim to fame, though it is not literary and belongs more rightly in the category of infamy. In the late thirteenth century, a certain Dominican friar named Robert of Reading delved too far into the texts in his search for truth. Not content with the Latin bible, he studied Greek and then Hebrew, determined to go as far back as he could, to the very source of his faith. From the Hebrew bible it seems he graduated to the Talmud, and thence to the Kabbala, the mystical teachings of Judaism. There is no record of what his brother friars thought of all this, or even where he found all these source materials. What *is* recorded is that he renounced Christianity, embraced Judaism, changed his name to Hagai, and married a Jewish wife.

It is true that Hagai of Reading does not have quite the same ring as Robert of Reading, but nevertheless the name rang loud and clear all over England at that time. So loud, in fact, that some chroniclers regard his conversion as the main trigger for the expulsion of the Jews from England in the year 1290—an expulsion that would last close to four hundred years.

Other chroniclers were not so eager to sanitize history. England, after all, was the home of the blood libel. Robert of Reading's seduction into infamy merely added a minor name to a far more glorious roster—the list of boy martyrs such as Hugh of Lincoln and William of Norwich, famed and adored for their murders by "the wicked Jewes."

The medieval imagination can never be accused of having lacked in gory detail. According to these chroniclers, the boys had been forcibly circumcised to purify them; their throats had been cut by a ritual slaughterer; they had been strung up by their heels and the slaughterer had held out a silver bowl to collect the life's blood pouring out of them; and then, as all good Christians of the time knew, that blood was used to make the matzos Jews ate for Passover. The boys had pleaded for mercy, calling on Christ to save them, and the wicked Jews had laughed at their pleas. Just as the Jews had murdered Christ, now they murdered His saints.

The Jews, of course, were foreign. That is, they'd only lived in England a couple of hundred years. They had come following the Norman Conquest of 1066, part of the new European influence in this primitive isle. By the twelfth and thirteenth centuries, when the blood libels gathered momentum, the Jews were double and triple taxed, their homes attacked and burned, their lives under constant threat. Londoners celebrated Richard I's coronation in 1189 by massacring Jews. In 1278, 278 were hanged for clipping coin—giving short weight; Christians guilty of the same offense were merely fined. City after city expelled the Jews. When the national expulsion decree came—get out of England by All Saints' Day of the year 1290, or be killed—it must have been almost a relief.

With that decree, England distinguished itself by being the first European country to expel the Jews. France followed suit soon after, and two hundred years later so did Spain, thus putting an end to the golden age of Jewish and Moslem culture centered in the south, and introducing a new dimension of darkness—the Inquisition.

None of this was common knowledge in twentieth-century England. It was in none of the history books we studied at school. It was a separate history, one never covered in any books except Jewish ones, and then only the most academic. Nobody ever mentioned it, neither Jew nor non-Jew. It had a kind of underground existence that was entirely at odds with England's post–World War Two image of itself flying high the brave banner against despotism and dictatorship. So that when I discovered it, a precocious Jewish twelve-year-old reading too widely for my age, it made the ground beneath my feet seem suddenly insubstantial. The once-comforting Victorian Gothic red brick of Reading's town library became abruptly cold and threatening. What had seemed solid and secure—my existence in England—became more like a shaky rope bridge over an unknown chasm.

Not that the idea of expulsion was new to me. After all, people were always getting banished in history and fairy tales, though it's true they were usually lords and knights. Legends grew up around them, romantic tales of bravery and love, longing and derring-do. To be banished was in itself an honorable distinction.

But expelled? The very word had none of the soft, lingering effect of banishment. It came out hard, almost spat out, harsh and uncompromising. You could be expelled from school—one girl in our class had been expelled for stealing—and that was the end for you. You were branded, unutterably shamed, forced out of the secure world into a world where no good school would want you. Nobody could possibly want someone who'd done something so terrible as to be expelled.

And then to expel a whole group of people not for what they'd done, but for who they were? I sat in the library at a table by the history section and stared around me at all the English faces. No, of course they wouldn't want to expel me for being Jewish, not them. That had been long ago, another time. But not another country. If I'd been born eight centuries earlier, I would have been expelled simply because I was born to a Jewish mother and a Jewish father. Surely that sort of thing happened only in Germany? Not in civilized England.

I was stunned by the awareness that I could be either elevated or expelled because of something I had no control over—my birth.

I know now that England is a country where your status has always been determined by birth. That is the essence of the class system. Anti-Semitism creates an extra, outsider class, which is useful for deflecting attention from the system itself. But I didn't make the connection then; I couldn't, not at that age, not while I was still trying to be English. Besides, when you grow up with an undercurrent of anti-Semitism all around you, you take it for granted. You do your best not to notice it. It seems natural, nothing worth distinguishing. You learn, in other words, to ignore it.

Except for that one time in the library, I spent twenty years ignoring it.

OF course, the expulsion of the Jews was hundreds of years ago. Ancient history, for some. So what about today? After all, there are well over a quarter million Jews in England today. Some of them even have knighthoods and life peerages. Things have obviously changed.

Or become more subtle.

Like the time a new English acquaintance, a woman in her fifties, discovered I was Jewish. "Isn't that odd," she said, "I never realized that. You don't seem at all Jewish. In fact, I've only really known one other Jew." And she began to talk about a friend at school. They were friends for three years, until the other girl's family moved to a different town. "It was only after she'd left that I found out she was Jewish. Honestly, I was never aware of it. I never knew there was anything wrong with her."

As she herself would hasten to say, this was said with the best intentions. It was said to indicate that where others might think there was something wrong with that girl—"quite a nice girl, considering"—my acquaintance did not. But then of course she didn't *know.* And if she had?

When I was still properly English—or as proper as I ever managed to be—I would have taken her remark in good faith. You become very good at ignoring things if you're Jewish in England. The awareness of anti-Semitism can be repressed, denied, adjusted to, compensated for, there are a hundred and one psychological defense mechanisms against it.

"After all, why make such a *fuss* about it?" as the English say. As though millions of Jews hadn't been killed in Europe in the six years before I was born. "Why do they have to go on so about it?"

To "go on so about it" betrays, of course, a lack of class. As one of England's top literary critics, A. Alvarez, once put it: "Being Jewish in England is not quite polite. It's rather like dropping your 'h's when you speak."

And English Jews internalize that. Where American Jews speak out, act out, revel in, and even flaunt their Jewishness, English Jews tend to close in, retreat, as though living in a constant state of repressed anxiety about it. In that sense, they are being very English—trapped in passivity, unwilling to react, rock the boat, make a *fuss*.

After all, it's been only four hundred years since they were allowed back into England.

Oliver Cromwell knew what he was doing by letting them back. England was in a trade war with Holland, and Jews had helped make Dutch and Italian ports into the main international trading centers of the time. England needed traders. And despised them at the same time, as it still does.

The upper-class Briton looks down on trade as on a lower-class neighbor with an old shiny suit and frayed cuffs. The privileged educational enclaves of Oxford and Cambridge universities—known collectively as Oxbridge—simply ignore trade, training their students for higher things. Listen to the word "trade" uttered with an upper-class accent—drawn out, sneering, like William F. Buckley, Jr. uttering the word "idealism"—and you can hear the disdain.

Not that the Jews had much choice in the matter. They were traders and moneylenders because they were kept out of the professions, restricted in buying land, and forced into the only livelihoods remaining to them. The majority of English Jews are still store-owners, businessmen, and small manufacturers—"in trade," like Margaret Thatcher's father, a grocer.

Traditional Tories wrung their hands in despair when this grocer's daughter was elected to the highest office in the land. What was the party coming to, let alone the country? Margaret Thatcher, the epitome of middle classness, was everything establishment England abhors. How "common" she was! My dear, that accent! You could *hear* all those drearily earnest elocution lessons. And that dress! That total lack of any sense of noblesse oblige. That ruthless belief in bettering oneself the hard way.

And as though in sheer delight at having bested the traditionalists in the political field, Thatcher surrounded herself not only by non-Oxbridge men, but worse, by Jews. Good lord, at one time there were three of them—three!—in her cabinet. "They seem to be getting everywhere nowadays," you'd hear in the clubs along St James's. "One wonders what that bloody woman thinks she's doing."

"They" play English and remain silent. Perhaps it needed an American to see this phenomenon and give voice to it. And perhaps it was inevitable that this American be Philip Roth, the master of problematic Jewishness. Whatever, the closing section of his prize-winning novel *The Counterlife* is less fiction than superb reportage. To read it was to remember all the things I'd heard and yet not heard for all the years I'd lived in England.

Being Jewish, says Zuckerman's English wife in the novel, "is something they ought to have dropped because it's very boring, they're being so Jewish about it." And adds: "It is common parlance—and not necessarily anti-Semitic—for people to say 'Oh, such-and-such is frightfully Jewish . . .'."

I was Zuckerman and Zuckerman's wife at the same time. Deceived by my blond hair and Anglicized name, the English sometimes invite me into the general assumption: "They do get up your nose, though, don't they? They're so bloody sensitive about it." And on discovering that I too am Jewish, they inevitably fall back on the old saw: "I once had a very close friend who was a Jew, you know."

Yes, I want to reply, and I once had a pet white rabbit. But I don't say it—not in England. After all, one doesn't want to be rude. That wouldn't be playing the game.

In *The Counterlife,* Nathan Zuckerman, as is his habit, puts his finger on the matter. Under assault from open Jew baiters in a restaurant, and from his more subtle but still clearly Jew-baiting in-laws, he sees "a deep, insidious Establishment anti-Semitism that is latent and pervasive but that, among the mild, well-brought-up, generally self-concealing English, only the occasional misfit actually comes out with." Which is what makes it so difficult to counter.

"How enraging," thinks Zuckerman, "to blunder smilingly into people who want no part of you."

And writing now, I can understand why so few English Jews have written about this quietly stated, elusive anti-Semitism, always intimated rather than openly stated. Often, it is a matter of insinuation, with the intent in the intonation rather than the words used, in the sneering impatience with those who point it out, in the use of a phrase like "you people," or the condescending smile and lingering emphasis on the last word of "Oh, you're Jewish? How . . . uh, *interesting.*"

It makes you long for the plain old outspoken rabid sort of anti-Semitism, something you can easily identify and counter-attack. Sometimes it's the shock of the one revealing statement slipping out of a well-bred, sophisticated intellectual. Other times it's what Roth calls "the peculiarly immoderate, un-Englishmanlike Israel-loathing" that comes out at a dinner party at mention of the Mideast conflict. Most of the time it's just a slight sneer, a curl of the lip, as otherwise innocuous words take on a twist and a snap . . .

If you pay attention to it, it can drive you quite mad with frustration and rage. Which is why most English Jews don't.

THE powers of denial are rich and wondrous. I was the only Jew in a convent school, and so far as I remember, experienced no anti-Semitism there. Yes, of course the Jews killed Christ, but it was made clear that I was not held responsible for that. There was a great generosity in the school about my being Jewish, as though I was being forgiven for it. Since I was being as English as I knew how at the time, I took this in good faith. I was "the, uh . . . the *Hebrew* girl" to the nuns, who did their best to convert me until my parents got wind of it and put a stop to that.

You have to be English to understand why I, a Jew, was sent to a convent school. Reading was a small town, at that time still beyond the commuting periphery of London. It had two "good" schools for girls, at a time when all "good" education in England was still sex segregated. One was the Abbey, which took only Church of England pupils. No Catholics, no Jews. The other was the Convent, which took a considerable number of Anglican pupils so that it could get supplementary government funding, and which was happy to take in a Jew. There was always the chance of converting me.

My parents wanted what all parents want for their children—a good education. They had the option of sending me to a boarding school, but neither I nor they wanted that. So if not the Abbey, then the Convent. It didn't seem such a difficult decision; my mother had been schooled in a convent in her home town of Drogheda, halfway between Dublin and the border with Northern Ireland. The nuns there provided the only education going.

Being the only Jew in a convent school was an education in independent thinking. That is, an education in outsiderness. I was the one who stood while all the others knelt, twice a day, in prayer assembly. The one who came to school with strange and exotic foods during Passover. The one who got Jewish holidays off as well as Catholic ones. The one who was different.

For lack of a better option, I learned to dramatize this difference, using it to my advantage. I asked awkward questions in religion classes, to everyone's delight except that of the teacher. I resolved religious disputes between other pupils since I, the outsider, was clearly more objective. I used my being an outsider and at the same time I covered it up, trying to be "one of the girls" and wondering why I never quite fit.

If there were any discussions in school of Fagin or Shylock,

I don't remember them. I do remember concentrating on "Do we not bleed" to the exclusion of the rest of Shylock's role in *The Merchant of Venice*—written, incidentally, at a time when the Jews were still expelled from England. And I skipped lightly through *Oliver Twist* and looked for other, less unsettling Dickens novels. In this, I was being very English, practicing the art of selective attention. It never occurred to me that there was no English Malamud, no Roth, no Bellow or Potok, no Jews who wrote about Jewish life. If there had been, I wouldn't have wanted to know. Being Jewish was something to be played down, not written about. There was enough about Jews already in English literature.

It was left to George Orwell, writing in 1945, the year I was born, to point out "a perceptible anti-Semitic strain in English literature from Chaucer onwards." In fact, he said, anti-Semitism in England "has always been pretty widespread." Beyond the obvious Jew baiting of Pound, Belloc, and Chesterton (for whom Jews "tended to be" either traitors or tyrants), Orwell also fingered Shakespeare, Thackeray, G. B. Shaw, H. G. Wells, T. S. Eliot, and Aldous Huxley. Since Orwell was not Jewish, nobody could accuse him of being oversensitive. Instead, his essay on English anti-Semitism was simply ignored. Again, that fine art of selective attention.

True, his timing may not have been the best. Nobody wanted to know about anti-Semitism in England after World War Two, not least because the Jews suddenly had the temerity to start killing English soldiers in Palestine, claiming a state on the basis of that absurd declaration by that damn fool Balfour in 1917 and making an awful fuss, just as they always do, about Hitler and so on. Anyone would think they were the only ones who suffered casualties in the war, damn it.

Yes, England fought the Gerries in World War Two—that friendly, familiar term, Gerries, as though they were just jolly good chaps who happened to be on the other side, rather than Nazis. A generation later, the swastika is everywhere. Doodled on schoolbooks by bored students, sewn onto punk costumes in the early eighties, displayed on armbands and banners at football games.

Imagine if an American football team was nicknamed "The Yids," like Tottenham Hotspur in England. There'd be a national outcry, of course. It would be all over the network news. Editorials, demonstrations, boycotts, pressures of all sorts. A national debate over whether to close down the team or simply ban the fans. The ACLU waving the banner of free speech. The president advocating strong measures. . . .

I don't know how it would be resolved, but I do know one thing: No way would it be passed over in silence. No way would anyone say "it's harmless." And no way would anyone suggest, "don't make a fuss."

I made no fuss the time I was nearly expelled from school. When I raised my hand to ask Sister Dymphna why we couldn't study the reproductive system of the rabbit, was I trying for escape even then?

Escape from boredom, certainly. My rabbit was splayed obscenely open in front of me, legs pegged to the four corners of a tray. It was a sorry symphony of gray and white.

Sister Dymphna, the biology teacher, loomed massively over it all. I now realize she had a severe thyroid problem, which meant that, already tall, she was also massive, with triple chins that shook when she spoke, hairs sprouting at odd angles from her face, and a smell very like that of peas run to seed and sprouted. And for the fourth week running, she had assigned us the alimentary canal of the rabbit.

I knew all I ever wanted to know about the alimentary canal of the rabbit. I could trace the progress of food from mouth to esophagus, down the gullet to the stomach, past the biological stations of the cross—pancreas, liver, kidneys, small intestine, large intestine, rectum, and . . . out. The word "anus" was not used in the convent.

The other girls had neatly picked their cadavers apart, each detail laid along the side of the tray and labeled for inspection. They were making their rabbits into diagrams. I had made mine into a mass of slush. I raised my hand and asked my question.

There was a silence. A long silence. In it, I had time to wonder where that question had come from. I hadn't prepared it; it had just come out. At fourteen, I cared as little about the reproduction of the rabbit as I did about its digestion.

"Stand up, girl."

The accused must stand in the dock for sentencing. The mannish voice trembled under the weight of this awful circumstance.

"You are an evil girl," said Dymphna, voice heavy with portentousness. "An evil girl." She paused, waiting for the full impact of those words to take effect. "You know that this is a convent, and that we cannot teach such things here. Come out to the front of the class."

I walked up to the spot she indicated with her finger, just in front of her. She towered over me. And as I stood there she seemed to expand, like a hot-air balloon. The bigger she got, the redder her face became, until it seemed as though she would explode from the force of it and die in a burst of spontaneous combustion like Mr. Krook in Dickens's *Bleak House*, leaving only an evil-smelling viscous ooze spread over the floor.

I noted with interest that my knees shook, just as books said they did when someone was terrified. Dymphna took one more deep breath, became as big and as red as it seemed she could possibly be without exploding, and uttered her judgement:

"Until this day, I considered you a poor unfortunate pagan, one whose soul might yet be saved, one of those unfortunate millions bound for the emptiness of Limbo unless they could see the light. But now I know the truth. You have had a chance to see the light. You have had ample chance. We have done all we could for you in this school. And still you have rejected it. You have knowingly rejected it. If it were out of ignorance, you would go to Limbo, along with all those other unfortunate souls. But in your case, it is Evil that has led you to reject the light. And this means that you are condemned to Eternal Hell. Yes, for this you will go to Hell."

To hell? To fires and pitchforks and tortures? To the eternally damned and hopeless? In that case, I reasoned, there was nothing more to lose. And knowing that, though I was still cowed by the sheer immensity of her, I suddenly found the courage of the insulted.

I stood straighter, looked into that beet-red face, and even as I said the words, was amazed at the very fact that I was saying them:

"If I go to Hell, Sister, then I will meet you there."

There was a faint gasp of shock from the class behind me. A look of stunned amazement on Dymphna's face. A moment when everything seemed frozen, as though she and I were about to be transported in a flash to her Hell, there to continue our confrontation. I saw us surrounded by flames. Red and orange and gold and purple flickered over our faces as our ears filled with the screams of the damned. And I was content. So long as she was there too, I was content.

A huge hand reached out and grabbed me by the back of my collar, practically lifting me off my feet. I was dragged out of the classroom, feet scrambling to keep more or less upright. I'd never realized that such a massively flabby body could have such strength. She dragged me up the wooden stairs from the biology lab, along the green linoleum of the narrow upstairs corridor, down the wooden stairs by the assembly hall, along the green linoleum of another narrow corridor, up another flight of wooden stairs, and along the final wide corridor leading to the Holy of Holies at the end: the headmistress's study.

I fought and scrambled and struggled and kicked. I scratched and clawed. I would have bitten were the idea of biting into that mass of flesh not so revolting. But Dymphna kept her hold on me and burst straight through the door.

The headmistress rose bolt upright from her desk, her face even whiter than usual. How could anyone—anyone at all—burst into her room like this, without even knocking? She surveyed the scene—Dymphna swollen and red with anger, me disheveled and out of breath—with obvious distaste.

"And what is the meaning of this?" she said, all dignity in the face of emotion run riot. "Sister Dymphna, kindly release that girl. Stand up straight, girl. Tidy yourself. Now, an explanation, if you please."

Dymphna poured out her tale of woe. I barely took in what she was saying. I'd only been in this room once before, when the headmistress had smilingly assured my parents that the Convent would not only do its utmost to give me the best of educations but would also of course respect children from other faiths. The smile had seemed false then, the woman grim and unyielding behind the smile. She looked far grimmer now.

"I presume you understand that there is no possibility of your remaining in this school after this shameful display. Never, in all my years of teaching, have I heard of such disrespect. I will not even consider the larger issues of heresy and evil. There is no need. You will be expelled from this school."

No way. I wanted revenge, and to achieve revenge I had to stay. Revenge binds the insulter and the insulted. For better or for worse—I didn't care which. I wanted, above all, to be justified.

"In that case, Sister, I shall have to tell my parents exactly what Sister Dymphna said to me."

A stunned silence. I pressed my advantage. "I'm sure they would tell a lot of other people. And soon the whole town would know that a nun in this convent told a Jewish girl that she was a pagan and was going to Hell."

Dymphna's black mass shook as she sputtered, groping for words that were beyond her. The headmistress flushed; it was quick, a faint tinge of pink in the cheeks and on the forehead, but enough. She took a deep breath and turned, looking out the window at the red brick building that housed the laboratory. Her hands were clasped tightly behind her back, knuckles white with tension.

Dymphna was sent back to the class. I was asked to sit down. Of course I understood that Sister Dymphna was under tremendous pressure. That teaching was a very demanding profession. That we all say things we don't mean on occasion. That of course there was no question of my leaving the school. So long as I wished to stay, they would be delighted. A good student like myself. . . .

I played the game and accepted her terms, knowing as I did so that this was a Pyrrhic victory. I'd heard that victory was sweet, but this one wasn't. It couldn't be. Even the largest victories over prejudice never are, let alone the ones so small that they have to be won by children.

FRIENDLY TOYS

I can't remember when I saw my first golliwog. It's like trying to remember when you saw your first Raggedy Ann. Every child, it seemed, had one at some time or another. We cuddled up with them at night, pulled their hair by day, flung them across the room in tantrums, trampled on them and pummeled them, and still they smiled back at us—big red smile, bright white eyes, indestructible.

They were simple toys, inexpensive to make. Good for postwar Britain. A round stuffed shape for the body, a smaller round for the head, four sausage shapes for the arms and legs, and thick wool for the hair, preferably wool that had already been knitted and then unraveled, to give it the right kinky look.

The hair had to be kinky, of course, because golliwogs were black.

Nobody's quite sure which came first, the doll or the word *wog,* one of the more infamous linguistic inventions of the British Empire. *The Oxford English Dictionary* maintains that it's used to refer to all foreigners, but the *O.E.D.* is being politely evasive. In fact it was used to refer only to nonwhite foreigners—and since the English were not in the habit of encountering any foreigners unless forced to, let alone colored ones, it really referred to citizens of African and Asian member countries of the Empire.

Several generations of majors and colonels and captains—all inextricably middle class at home but the ruling elite abroad—

came back to tell wide-eyed grandchildren about their adventures among the wogs. Gordon of Khartoum was one of the favorite stories: the British Custer, the lone white man, beleaguered and besieged, defending the fort against a whole bloody army of them rushing up the hill, eyes and teeth flashing white against coal black skin. A load of bloody banshees, screaming maniacally, fit to scare the living daylights out of you. There were good wogs and bad wogs, mind you—had to be fair, you know, couldn't lump them all together. The good ones were charming people, really, quite childlike once you got the trick of handling them. Had to show them who's master, of course. Don't know how to do a damn thing, those wogs. Can't trust them, you know. Can't get anything at all done unless you stand over them. Bloody wogs.

Good old England, besieged by her own sense of duty, an island of civilization afloat in a sea of wogdom. It was as though the Statue of Liberty were to float out of New York harbor, torch bobbing out of the water, bearing the message to peoples entirely unable to perceive pride and freedom in the image of a lady floating on her back.

For those still in any doubt as to the matter, incidentally, the American equivalent of "bloody wogs" is "damn niggers."

I left an England that was still almost solidly white. Some West Indians had made it to those hallowed shores—few enough, at the time, for them to be considered exotic and interesting. Tall, delicately colored, with lilting accents, their slang was already beginning to infiltrate. "Put a tiger in your tank," said Esso, the forerunner of today's Exxon, and the British did, all unaware that the phrase was West Indian slang for sexual arousal.

The Empire was fast coming apart at the time, as though a carefully knit tea cosy covering the world had come unraveled. But the English were slow to realize that. Poor England, still besieged by a sense of innate superiority, where white equaled civilization and black equaled natives, wogs, and anarchy. All nice enough, of course, when the Queen went to visit and they put on their native dances for her. A bit much with all those naked breasts flying around, but noblesse oblige and all that. You had to keep the natives happy.

And the kids happy too. So easy to make a golliwog: Just sew on big white buttons for the eyes, a piece of red felt cut into a crescent for the mouth, and there you have it, the perfect wog, amenable, maltreatable, cuddly, unthreatening, brought down to size and tucked up with the kids to keep them company in the dark; nine o'clock and all's well with the world and Britannia still rules the waves.

Other dolls had names. There was Mary, who'd lost both arms and both eyes and nearly all her hair before I'd agree to consign her to oblivion. And Edward, my teddy bear, who smelled much as a real bear smells by the time they wrested him away from me. But a golliwog was simply a golliwog, a nameless, pervasive presence.

"She's making white golliwogs for sale in color-prejudice trouble spots," said a character in Joe Orton's sixties play, *What the Butler Saw.* Rocking and shocking the middle class was Orton's forte. To attack golliwogs was to attack all that was cuddliest and most innocent about England.

For sure, Orton collected the golliwog labels from the top of Robertson's jam jars just as I did in the fifties. If you saved enough of them you could send them in to Robertson's, the biggest jam-makers in England, and get a real enameled golliwog brooch in return, bright and shiny on its neat little pin. At first they were just plain golliwogs, natty in blue jackets and red pants, but then Robertson's had the bright idea of making them musical. Wogs, after all, have such a good sense of rhythm. So the golliwogs began to play trumpets and drums, cymbals and triangles, and soon, if you ate enough jam and sent in all your golliwog labels, you could accumulate a whole golliwog band of brooches.

Orton, with his highly developed sense of the absurd, must have reveled in it. If you weren't a Joe Orton, you participated in the absurd without being aware of it. I collected the brooches as they came in the mail, keeping them all in a Huntley and Palmer's biscuit tin with a bucolic country scene on the lid of lords and ladies dining al fresco under a willow tree—the kind of tin you can now find for a hundred dollars in a New York antique store.

But I never wore my brooches.

And I never saw anyone else wearing them.

Perhaps, after all, consciousness did glimmer, albeit unacknowledged. To acknowledge it would have made us all into Joe Ortons, masters of the violent absurd.

THE Empire struck back. From India, Pakistan, Uganda, Tanganyika, Guyana, Jamaica, Nigeria—from all those parts of the globe once colored deep pink in English atlases—citizens of Empire claimed their right to immigrate to the mother country. In the mid-sixties, the movement gained momentum; it continued through the seventies and, despite stricter immigration laws, on into the eighties. The popular press was full of talk of immigrants "flooding in," of "alien hordes" and "brown tidal waves."

And then there was the famous "swamping" statement in 1978: "You know, the British character has done so much for democracy, for law, and done so much throughout the world, that if there is a fear that it might be swamped, people are going to react and be rather hostile to those coming in. So, if you want good race relations, you have got to allay people's fears on numbers."

That was Margaret Thatcher, speaking on a prime-time political television program. It's a remark that will never be forgotten, and that she has never tried to soften or change. It also explains why England's colored minorities vote almost solidly Labour.

The "alien hordes" constitute all of four and one-half percent of England's 56 million population—about 2.4 million. Of these, ninety-six percent of those under eighteen were born in England. About half are of Indian and Pakistani origin, and a quarter are Afro-Caribbean. They include 1.5 million Muslims, about 300,000 Hindus, and about 300,000 Sikhs. (By way of comparison, there are some 300,000 Jews.) The English like their minorities small, and intend to keep them that way. Some by immigration control, others by violence.

"Paki bashing" became a popular pastime among white London working-class youths in the seventies. In some areas of London, young Asian women wash their hair every night; they have to, because their hair is full of spit, hurled on them from escalators or passing buses or open windows. Police only opened a classification for racial attacks in the late eighties; until then, they were classed together with all other assaults. The second year's count in certain parts of east London was up thirty percent from the first.

A report commissioned by the now-defunct Greater London Council just before it was disbanded by Margaret Thatcher drily cataloged some of the abuse:

"Racist name-calling; rubbish, rotten eggs, rotten tomatoes, excreta, etc., dumped in front of victims' doors; urinating through the letter boxes of victims; fireworks; burning materials and excreta pushed through letter boxes; door knocking; cutting telephone wires; kicking; punching; spitting at victims; serious physical assault; damage to property such as windows being broken, doors smashed, racist graffiti daubed on door or wall. Dogs, cars, and motorcycles are still being used to frighten black people. Shotguns and knives have also been used."

"They're taking our jobs" is one of the regular complaints. In fact, young colored Britons are twice as likely to be unemployed as whites, and those whose families come from Pakistan and Bangladesh, three times as likely. The most striking illustration of the fate of colored minorities in England is that of the Vietnamese boat people. While elsewhere they've prospered, in England they've foundered, to the extent that a Home Office report found it "difficult to identify any other refugee group arriving in any other Western country which has fared as badly."

In the States, for instance, ninety-four percent of children whose families come from India and Pakistan graduate high school (compared to eighty-seven percent of American whites). In England, these same ethnic groups have the highest dropout rate. As racism, poor housing, unemployment, and sweatshop working conditions mount up, so does the rate of heart disease: England's rate is one of the highest in the world, and that of its Asian population is higher still.

Many of the older generation, like Prafulla Mohanti, an Indian painter and writer who came to England in 1960, anticipated the old image of England—a decent, tolerant society where justice was for all. "A land of daffodils," wrote Mohanti, "where men wore bowler hats . . . there was no poverty and people were honest and fair."

I remember that England; that is, I remember being taught that it existed, and only vaguely sensing that it didn't. Mohanti had that fact literally pushed into his face: He was driven from his home in east London, attacked in parks, spat on in the street, and demeaned by the police when he turned to them for protection and redress.

"My beloved London," murmurs Rafi, the corrupt Pakistani politician visiting his son in London at the start of Hanif Kureishi's movie *Sammy and Rosie Get Laid.* He thinks of it as "the center of civilization—tolerant, intelligent." And as he dreams lasciviously of "hot buttered toast on a fork in front of an open fire, and cunty fingers," his taxi drives right into the beginning of a race riot.

I'D followed all this from outside England, and paid scant attention to it the times I'd been back on brief visits. I'd assumed, for instance, that Robertson's jams must have dropped their golliwog logo sometime in the late sixties. Certainly by the early seventies. After all, the whole awareness of race and race relations had changed radically over the past two decades. Surely no company so dependent on public goodwill could afford to retain such a clearly racist symbol.

But there is something about Margaret Thatcher's England that makes you question long-held assumptions, even ones you were barely conscious of. Now that I was in England for a longer stay, I could check things out. Which is why I stopped by the jam section of a large supermarket in north London one day. Just to make sure.

It was nostalgically reassuring to see so much jam. In the States, the closest equivalent for a long time was the saccharine slipperiness of grape jelly, and even though English jams have become terribly "in" with the latest wave of Anglophilia—and are known by the very proper name of preserves—they lack the comforting familiarity of ordinary, regular jam.

The jam section took up one whole aisle in the supermarket. Half of the jars were Robertson's, and all of them sported a large golliwog printed on their lids.

I picked up a jar of strawberry jam, the berries big and whole inside. The golliwog was a sleeker, more modern image than the old ones I grew up with—a streamlined version. Playing investigative consumer, I read the label:

"Enclose a stamped, self-addressed envelope, and send off for your FREE 'Great Golly Offers' leaflet which includes a wide range of Golly items for the whole family and details of our exclusive range of 16 Golly Brooches. Why not start your collection now!"

There was a stamp printed into the label, perforated edge and all. If you sent in three of these stamps, each of which showed a golliwog in some professional garb, and enclosed fifty pence, you'd get a brooch. That was undercutting their old rate, which used to be six paper golliwogs—but no money and also less work, since the old ones sat ready to be collected under the lid, while now you had to soak off the label to get the new ones.

I looked through all the Robertson's jars on the shelves. I found golliwog doctors, nurses, fishermen, policemen, lifeboatmen, butchers, astronauts, and finally, the one that begged to be bought—an American football player.

"Jam?" said the friends I was staying with when I got back with my purchases. They were newly devoted to health foods. "What are we going to do with jam?"

"Invite an American to tea," I said, as I waited for the label to soak off.

My "Great Golly Offers" leaflet arrived three weeks later. Sure enough, it offered sixteen different brooches, including the American footballer, the astronaut, a cowboy, a jogger, and a Canadian Mountie. It also offered a bewildering array of other golliwog items: T-shirts, sweatshirts, mugs, pens, knitting patterns for sweaters, jigsaws, key rings, stationery, salt and pepper sets, cutlery, tapestry kits, watches, aprons, tea cosies, tin trays, oven gloves, tea towels, teapots, rings, chains, hair clips, place mats, shopping bags, umbrellas, and, of course, "Cuddly Golly Dolls." And the most perplexing of all—a baseball cap "with its colourful Golly on the front."

That afternoon, I called the commercial director of Robertson's at the company headquarters in Manchester. He was happy to be of help.

"We send out about six or seven thousand little brooches a week," he said, his northern accent friendly and affable. "The first ones were introduced in 1928. We started off with plain ones, then we diversified. For years our most popular brooch was a little nurse. Then about two years ago, we put out an American footballer brooch—bloody ugly thing if you ask me—and would you believe, that's now the most popular one we've got. We send out about eight hundred a week just of that." And helpfully, he added, "American football's become a sort of status thing here, you know. I expect that's why."

He was so nice and chatty that it seemed a shame to raise the possibility that some people might be offended by the golliwog logo and brooches, but raise it I did.

"Oh yes," he said. "About every six years or so they get up a bit of a fuss. The slightly lunatic fringe, you know."

I suggested they might have a point worth considering.

His voice went official, losing its warm northern accent, as though he was reading a statement he'd given many times before to the press. "It's a child's toy, a doll. It is in no way intended to be a caricature or anything else. It was brought over from the States years ago, and we cannot accept that it is intended to be racist or anything else." He relaxed his tone again, having apparently reached the end of the formal statement. "The next thing they'll be saying is that Miss Piggy is an insult to pigs."

"Are you sure you want to draw that particular analogy?" I asked.

"Well, no, but you know what I mean. We don't pay any attention to these protests. They flare up and then die down again. We're used to it."

"Then you've made no changes as a result of the protests?"

"No. In fact if anything in the last couple of years, the redemption rate has gone up."

"Yet I notice you're not calling them golliwogs any more."

"Oh, we changed that." His voice went suddenly formal again. "The use of the word *golliwog* is derogatory, unpleasant, and can cause offense, and we did change it because of that. We changed it to *golly* in 1970."

"You just changed the name," I said.

"Just the name," he replied.

IF you're of Pakistani or Indian or Afro-Caribbean origin in England, you are highly visible. The color stands out, the way it does in New England or in Alaska. In the tradition of third-world immigrants to Western countries, England's colored minorities often work in highly visible jobs—the jobs nobody else wants. They're the drivers and ticket collectors on London Transport buses and underground trains. They staff government hospitals. They run half the corner grocery stores. The newspaper stalls. The railways. They have the temerity to be seen.

"Bloody cheek," says that aging civil servant of Empire. "All well and good when they stayed where they belong, know what I mean? But then to come here and claim they're British, and after all we've done for the little bastards too. Where would they be without us? That's what I want to know. Back in the bloody jungle, that's where. And now here they come, pretending to be British, pouring in the floodgates. I mean, damn it, someone's got to put a stop to it, you know. England won't be England if this goes on much longer."

"They."

They are all English citizens. The younger generations, born in England, speak perfectly accented English—not a trace of the lilting accents which caused so much fun and derision when I was still growing up in England, when Peter Sellers's imitation of an Indian accent was somehow better than the real thing. A few have made it as businessmen. Even fewer, in the arts.

Hanif Kureishi is the scriptwriter son of a Pakistani father and British mother. He never set foot in Pakistan until he was in his twenties. Overwhelmed by the size of his family there, by the difference of culture, by the expectations and hopes and disappointments on all sides, he only realized there, in Pakistan, how much he was a product of England. Even though in England, "at least once a day since I was five years old I had been racially abused."

"It is the British, the white British," he wrote after that visit, "who have to learn that being British isn't what it was. Now it is a more complex thing, involving new elements. So there must be a fresh new way of seeing Britain and the choices it faces, and a new way of being British after all this time. . . . The failure to

grasp this opportunity for a revitalized and broader self-defini-
tion in the face of a real failure to be human, will be more
insularity, schism, bitterness and catastrophe."

Two years later, his movie *Sammy and Rosie Get Laid*—a vivid,
energetic picture of the inner city in flames, of people searching
for love against a background of poverty, violence, and decay—
was released in England. It was greeted by extraordinarily vicious
personal attacks in the guise of criticism—so vicious that you
knew Kureishi had touched a deep, vulnerable nerve.

When I called him, he seemed surprised that anyone he
didn't already know would still want to talk to him. He was
working on a new script about the rich, he said. So in a mood of
ostentatious absurdity, we decided to meet for tea at the Ritz, on
Piccadilly.

I arrived five minutes late to find him slouched disconso-
lately against an ornate marble table just inside the entrance, a
slight young man looking slighted. "They won't let me in," he
said.

I gave an inward groan—racism at the Ritz? "Why not?" I
asked.

He looked down. "I'm wearing jeans."

So we went along Piccadilly to Fortnum and Mason, where
we ordered cucumber and cress sandwiches. What else, I reasoned, would you order for tea in such a place? But the moment
they arrived, neatly cut into triangles with the crusts sliced off,
I remembered making them myself one summer when I was
working in a hotel on the Thames. It wasn't a good place to work,
and those of us on the waitress shift expressed it by spitting in
the sandwiches as we prepared the afternoon teas—the hidden
revenge of the powerless.

Kureishi gave me an odd look, and put down his sandwich.
"I wish you hadn't remembered that," he said.

I put mine down too. I also wished I hadn't.

So in the oddly antiseptic tearoom of Fortnum's, with its

white tiles and crisp white and green wallpaper, among the hair-sprayed ladies eating their cucumber and cress sandwiches, at least some of which, I could swear, had been spat in, we sipped our Earl Grey tea and looked at the rich. It seemed a perfect irony considering Kureishi's article in *The Guardian* a few days before.

"England seems to have become a squalid, ugly and uncomfortable place," he'd written, in a tone radically different from his measured plea of a couple of years before. "For some reason I am starting to feel that it is an intolerant, homophobic, narrow-minded, authoritarian rat hole run by vicious, suburban-minded, materialistic philistines who think democracy is constituted by the selling of a few council houses and shares."

An all-out attack on Thatcherism, it was an article that seemed to despair of England. "The best and most sensible are leaving if they can afford to."

"Does that mean you're leaving too?" I asked.

"Oh no," he said, "I wouldn't leave. England's been very good to me."

I looked up in surprise. He almost smiled. "Yes, it's given me my venom, and that's what keeps me writing."

It was, of course, a writer's answer, and true. There's been plenty of acclaim for Kureishi alongside the criticism, but despite the issues of *Granta* and the movies, the contracts and the contacts, he has those familiar creases of anxiety on his forehead and around his eyes, the look that says he can never be quite sure, he can never quite let down his guard, he can never, ever, take things for granted. Least of all his Englishness.

LIKE any self-respecting adult, I am quite capable of spending a whole afternoon in a toy store, so I gave myself plenty of time when I went down to Hamley's on Regent Street. Hamley's is the F. A. O. Schwartz of London, and like F. A. O. Schwartz, there aren't too many children in it. Playing with toys is one thing, buying them is another; adults reserve that prerogative for themselves.

A young man and woman wearing Hamley's jackets stood just inside the entrance, engrossed in a conversation that had her twining ringlets in her long blond hair. In front of them, a counter display of a new "educational" game was in a state of pristine neatness, having attracted no interest all day. It seemed a shame to interrupt the conversation, but I was there with a mission.

"Excuse me," I said, "do you have golliwogs?"

The girl stared at me with wide-open eyes. "Oh, we're not meant to use that word."

"Which word?"

"The word you just used," said the young man.

"You mean *golliwogs?*"

They both nodded. "Christine said that word last year," said the girl, "and it turned out the man she used it to was a reporter pretending not to be one, and she got put in the paper for it."

Getting put in the paper was clearly something on the order of getting put in jail. English journalists are held in much lower repute than their favored American counterparts; often you'd imagine they were Satan incarnate. I wanted to ask what happened to Christine after she got put in the paper, but feared revealing myself as another one of those underhanded reporters.

"Well, what am I meant to call them if not golliwogs?" I asked.

"Gollies," she said.

"Do you have any gollies, then?"

"I don't know," said the young man, "but if we do, they're up on the third floor."

It took me some time to reach the third floor, since I kept getting waylaid by toys. I stood fascinated by a pit full of mechanical dogs—poodles and pooches, Saint Bernards and sausage dogs, spaniels and just plain mutts, all thrown in and switched on together. Ears, heads, tongues, legs, tails, backsides—everything waggled. The creatures crawled all over each other, piling up in a wiggling heap that began to look like an obscene orgy of helpless canine passion.

"Do you think this is suitable for children?" I said.

The saleswoman gave me a blank look.

"I'm really looking for golliwogs," I confessed.

She didn't seem to think there was anything odd about that word. Perhaps she didn't know Christine. "They're up with the cuddlies," she replied, "on the next floor."

I'd never seen so many teddy bears gathered together in one place. Or fluffy pooches. Or stuffed pandas. At the end of an aisle full of absurdly giant ladybirds laid out in long rows, I managed to get the attention of a young saleswoman intent on ignoring all customers.

"Excuse me, where can I find a golliwog?"

"A golliwog," she said reflectively. Christine had evidently not worked on this floor either. "I don't know if we have any right now. There was a bit of a fuss some time ago, and I think we stopped carrying them temporarily."

"When will you have them again?"

"I don't know."

"Who would know, do you think?"

She shrugged. "You can try that lady over there."

That lady over there was an older woman, evidently a senior saleswoman. I waylaid her among the teddy bears. "Oh, of course we have them," she said. "We just don't put them on display anymore, but we do have them behind the counter. There was all that fuss about them not long ago, you know—people objected, said they were racist and all that. Daft, if you ask me. A lot of fuss about nothing. They're only children's toys. I don't know why people have to take everything so seriously."

She led me over to the counter, talking as we went. "In fact," she said, "I can tell you there was a dark gentleman here from America a few weeks ago, and he bought half a dozen of them. He didn't seem to think there was anything wrong with them at all. A very nice gentleman he was too, considering."

I didn't know if she meant "considering that he was American" or "considering that he was black."

She looked around behind the counter for a while, but came up shaking her head. "Now isn't that a shame?" she said. "I know we had them here two weeks ago. We must have sold out. I'm sure there's more on order if you want to come back. If not, we've got some wonderful new dolls in."

No, I said, it had to be a golliwog, and maybe the floor manager could tell me when they'd be in. She pointed out the floor manager, a young dark-suited woman whom I caught up with by a corner shelf of rather sad pink piglets.

"What do these do?" I asked.

She sighed. "They squeak when you squeeze them."

I squeezed one. Even the squeak was sad. I asked about the golliwog situation. She sighed again.

"Well, it's all a bit unclear at the moment," she said. "I think we'll have them back in soon, but I'm not sure exactly when. Every now and again there's a fuss. We have to take them off the shelves, and then it takes a few weeks to put them back on again. But if you try again next month, I'm sure we'll have them back in."

I felt curiously let down, as though I'd actually wanted to buy one of those elusive golliwogs. With black and white on my mind, I bought a miniature giant panda for my friends' one-year-old son.

The senior saleswoman smiled sympathetically as she rang up the purchase on the cash register. "So sorry about the golliwog," she said. "They're such friendly toys, aren't they?"

"Yes, aren't they?" I said with the kind of automatic politeness that becomes second nature in England. And as I watched her wrap the panda, I wondered if I hadn't overreacted. After all, they were right: A golliwog was only a toy.

I knew the fallacy the moment I thought it. Racial slurs can be rationalized as "only a joke." Vandalism and hooliganism as "only high spirits." Golliwogs as "only a toy." Yet in England today, people are being attacked and killed because they are "wogs." They are even being attacked and killed because they are football fans. In a troubled society, jokes and toys and high spirits and games become very serious. Deadly serious. Which is why, the following weekend, I decided to go to a football game.

OPERATION LION

IT was close to halftime, and Arsenal was losing one to nothing. Pete, seated behind me, was not pleased.

"You stupid great bastard."

"You bleedin' black git."

"You dumb Irish cunt."

The curses came pouring out of him as player after player flubbed the ball. They rang mightily in my left ear, then hurled on past, leaving me momentarily deaf. No finesse here, just good solid Anglo-Saxon words like *git*. It's defined in *The Oxford English Dictionary* as a worthless person, but only derives its true force as an insult when yelled with a real London accent—not "Master piece Theatre" upper class, but street London, with the *g* rock hard and the *t* swallowed in a glottal stop.

"Jee-zus," Pete screamed, thumping my shoulder in frustration as Arsenal flubbed another attack on the goal. "You fuckin' idiots. You couldn't score in a brothel!"

I rubbed my shoulder demonstratively.

"Oh I'm sorry, love. I get a bit carried away, if you know what I mean. You all right, then?" He turned to his mates sitting either side of him. "Got to look after her, you know. She's from New York."

She's from New York, and she's forgotten about English football, better known in America as soccer. She's used to the family atmosphere of the baseball game, where everyone's a manager and each play is calmly discussed, where the worst that happens to the visiting team is a deadly silence when they score. Where play stops when a beach ball is thrown onto the field and the television cameras deliberately avoid showing it so as not to encourage such rowdy behavior. And now she thinks about it, there's not many families here. Not many women at all. Or young children. Or blacks. In fact the crowd of thirty-five thousand packed into a structure the size of a tiny spring-training stadium in Florida consists almost entirely of young white men aged fifteen to thirty. All with lusty lungs for shouting and cursing, and lusty bellies filled with strong English ale. Forget about English fair play—this is football, and a huge ringing chorus of boos greets the opposing team the moment they set foot on the field.

We're in the Arsenal Stadium in north London. My friend Hugh has come with me, and I'm grateful for it. He's big. Arsenal is playing Manchester United, and since the two teams are vying for the lead in the first division, this win will make a big difference for either side.

Since being American clearly gets me preferential treatment, I don't tell Pete and his mates, Dennis and Mike, that I'm originally English. They probably wouldn't believe me, in any case, not with my mid-Atlantic accent. I can't even understand what the fans are chanting, and Pete and the others have been sweetly helpful ever since I introduced myself, translating the chants and explaining the offside rules I'd forgotten. Sweetly helpful, that is, until a tight play comes up, when they cut off in midsentence to shout:

"Yah, you can't even find the balls between your bleeding legs!"

Mike shrugs half-apologetically when I catch his eye. "Welcome to football," he says. And grins.

I like these kids. Their enthusiasm is fun. The vigor with which they express it is alive, free of the repression that clamps down on most of England. They're eighteen and nineteen, uneducated, and already on the dole or stuck in dead-end jobs, but for the space of a Saturday afternoon they can forget all that and openly, loudly, and raucously enjoy themselves. It's infectious, and though I'm not the biggest fan football's ever seen, I'll soon be yelling and waving and cheering too.

No holding back here. This is mainly a working-class crowd, uninterested in the stifling niceties of upper- and middle-class life. This is another England—the England ignored or conveniently forgotten by Anglophiles, who find it hard to reconcile their upper-class fantasies with lower-class reality. And that is exactly what attracts me. This is real. There is no masking.

I don't have to think about my words or consider if they're in place, worry about behaving properly or saying the wrong thing—dropping a brick on a foot I couldn't even see. There's no embarrassment here. That's the pleasure of it, and that's why the stadium is crammed. The emotional restrictiveness of being English breaks down here. You can let go.

Within limits, that is. This is football in the eighties, and there's a ring of uniformed police around the pitch, spaced about five yards apart from each other. Both teams' colors are red and white, and the stadium would be a sea of red and white if it weren't for the lines of navy-blue police uniforms. They circle the terraces behind the goals at each end of the pitch.

Fans pay four pounds for the privilege of standing on one of these terraces—huge, stepped-concrete structures, open to the sky. You have to come early to get a good place on a terrace, and once you've found it you can't leave. You need a strong bladder, or a willingness to stand on wet concrete pungent with urine.

Both terraces are packed—one end with Arsenal fans, cheering and jeering, the other with Manchester United fans who are just as loud. Chanted insults are traded back and forth the length of the pitch, like calls to arms trumpeted by medieval armies facing each other across a field of battle. A huge inflatable banana gets big play in the Arsenal terrace. It's raised high and jiggled up and down whenever Manchester's star player nears the goal. A chorus of monkey noises goes up, and the fans start jumping up and down and scratching under their arms. The player is black.

Either side of the pitch is lined with higher-priced stands, where, despite the name, you sit. The stands are not strictly segregated, apparently on the theory that those with a little more money are less prone to violence. We're seated at one end, right up beside the Manchester United terrace, where the thousands of fans who've followed their team south are penned in between high steel fences—crowd-control fences like those at Sheffield, where a year later, ninety-three fans would be crushed to death against the thick wire mesh. Empty concrete strips border the terrace, deliberately fenced off to act as no-man's-land. The idea is to keep opposing fans apart. Units of policemen stand in the otherwise empty strips. Their very presence seems like a challenge.

Suddenly there's an Arsenal attack—a pass, another pass, a header towards the goal, then another that slips in past the goalie. The stadium goes wild. I hardly register the goal being scored before Pete and Mike and Dennis behind me are standing on their seats, swaying, jumping up and down and stomping, gyrating their pelvises and making huge "fuck you" signs with their arms. They're not looking at the pitch. They're paying no attention to the players. They're focused entirely on the Manchester United terrace just a few yards away from us.

"Fuck you!"

"Yer stupid lot of wankers!"

"Manchester sucks!"

Dennis loses his balance, grabs my shoulder, straightens himself again and keeps right on. It's like some horribly stereotyped primitive tribal dance. Pelvises working and eyes glazed, fists punching the air and chants spat into the ether, it's some combination of war and fertility ritual, and apparently just as heady.

Penned behind their fences, the Manchester supporters respond in kind, spurring the Arsenal fans to more contortions. Pete is bouncing up and down on his seat. He's wearing huge, heavy work boots. I hear the seat crack. The police are all on their feet now. Poker-faced, they move in slightly, threatening. The referees rush to get the game started again. The ball goes into play; somebody gets in a good pass; elsewhere in the stands the crowd cheers it; the victory moment passes.

Pete and Mike and Dennis and dozens of others behind them settle back into their seats, flushed and panting and pleased with themselves, still muttering about northern gits and bastards and cunts, and take up the chant that's now sweeping over the Arsenal terrace and stands.

"Here we go, here we go, here we go . . ." they chant. The tune, disconcertingly, is "The Stars and Stripes Forever."

Beside me, Hugh visibly untenses.

So do the police. For now.

AT first, it had seemed like football as it used to be. We had joined the streams of people walking towards the stadium through the narrow streets lined with drab little two-story terrace houses, the kind of houses where people hunch around the fire in the front parlor and delay going to the bathroom because it's so cold out there, basically just a shed built onto the back of the house. Houses with flights of porcelain ducks on the walls, and a portrait of the Queen, and a fence in the back garden just high enough for privacy, just low enough for housewives to stand and chat over as they wonder whether to take in the washing now or whether to risk it for another half hour before it starts raining again.

The streets surrounding the stadium were packed. Hawkers sold programs, team buttons, hats, scarves—the scarves purely for identification, so flimsy they'd hardly keep out the slightest draft. Everyone seemed in a good mood. Genial. Comfortable. At first I didn't even notice the video cameras set on the roofs of some of the houses, pointed into the street. Police cameras.

I bought a portion of chips in a local fish-and-chip shop,

drenched them in vinegar, and was sharing them with Hugh when I saw the mounted police riding through the crowd. Both horses and riders wore riot gear—the helmeted riders in luminous green capes, the horses with huge reinforced plastic eye shields. They rode up and down in pairs, slowly, but the mood was so friendly and excited that the meaning of their presence didn't quite register.

We went into the stadium about half an hour before kick-off time. There were separate turnstiles for the terraces and the stands, and a lot of police by the turnstiles. They were frisking everyone who went onto the terraces. Occasionally, they'd take one or two fans aside altogether and frisk them far more thoroughly. The frisking was quick, efficient, polite, and insistent. And necessary.

The list of weapons found on football fans in the last few years includes the following:

Sharpened coins, bottles, bricks, catapults, lumps of concrete, razor blades, sheath knives, spring-loaded spikes, flares, plastic lemons filled with ammonia, stones, cans, smoke bombs, tear-gas grenades, hammers, machetes, blackjacks, surgical scalpels, knuckledusters, firecrackers, iron bars, petrol bombs, studded maces, spiked balls and chains, and darts.

For some reason, the darts are the weapon that gets to me most. It's the horror-movie nightmare of something so familiar becoming so threatening. A pub game suddenly becomes lethal. It reminds me of kneecapping in Northern Ireland: A savage form of revenge where you drill through a man's kneecap with a Black and Decker drill. I don't know why Black and Decker. I suppose even terrorists have brand loyalties.

PERHAPS the conflict in Northern Ireland has taken its toll on England. More likely, football violence is a reaction to the prim properness of Margaret Thatcher's determinedly middle-class regime, which has created legions of permanently unemployed young working-class men with lots of energy and lots of aggression, and no way to express it. They never subscribed to the rigid, formulaic politeness of English middle-class life—a politeness motivated less by consideration of others than by the will to repress. In a sense, football violence is a huge, obscene gesture directed at the ruling classes, at the rigid structure of English society. It is a working-class howl, and, like most howls of the powerless, it ends up hurting them more than anyone else.

A couple of days earlier, I'd spent eight hours in the morgue of *The Times,* going through the clippings on football violence in the last ten years. The morgue—the old journalistic term for the archive—was in a basement of the new *Times* complex in Wapping, part of London's renovated Docklands area.

The complex is known as "Fortress Wapping." Surrounded by guarded metal fences, electronic gates and cameras, it's clearly designed to withstand a siege. Which it has. When the *Times* owner, newspaper magnate Rupert Murdoch, ran head to head against the printers' unions, he transferred his entire operation from Fleet Street to Wapping, fortified the complex, and went on publishing without the unions. The picketing turned ugly, but Murdoch won. The picket lines have long gone, but the nickname "Fortress Wapping" remains. And security is still tight.

Reporter friends more or less smuggled me in there. Inevitably, I felt like a spy who'd infiltrated the defenses. Considering my purpose, the atmosphere seemed appropriate.

The sheer accumulation of violent fact was exhausting. Darts have been thrown at opposing goalies and at referees. Opposing players have been squirted with ammonia as they came onto the field. Referees and linesmen have been beaten up by fans. Bottles, sharpened coins, and bricks have been hurled at players. But all that's nothing compared to what opposing fans have done to each other.

A brief sample:

In January 1986, a bus full of supporters of Millwall, a London team, was returning to London after an away game in the north. It stopped at a motorway service station just as two buses of Newcastle United fans pulled in. Millwall had played Sunderland, not Newcastle, that day, but thirty Millwall fans nevertheless went crazy. They trashed the cafeteria, then leaped on a Newcastle fan, twenty-seven-year-old geologist Alan Price, as he stepped out of a phone box after calling his father. They beat him to a pulp and then scattered business cards over him—printed, embossed cards reading, "Congratulations, you have just met the Bushwhackers."

Millwall had lost their match that day; Newcastle had won.

In October 1986, nineteen-year-old Ken Burns had the temerity to shout "Up West Ham" in the face of Millwall supporters on a rampage through the West End after a Millwall–West Ham game. They chased him into the Embankment tube station and stabbed him six times. He died on the way to the hospital.

West Ham had won 2–1.

In May 1985, Liverpool United fans attacked fans of Turin's Juventus team in the Heysel Stadium in Brussels just before the start of a European Cup final game. As the opposing fans fought a pitched battle, throwing bottles and bricks, those below them on the terraces panicked and crushed forward. A retaining wall collapsed. The Liverpool fans pressed their attack. Thirty-nine people were trampled and suffocated to death. Four hundred and fifty were injured. Twenty-six Liverpool fans were eventually indicted on manslaughter charges in Brussels.

The game was played, and Liverpool lost 0–1.

After Heysel, English football clubs were banned from Europe, where football violence is known as "the English disease." The national team could still compete, but organized fans were not allowed to travel with them. Now, three years later, England was to meet Germany in the European Cup. Among the T-shirts on sale outside Arsenal Stadium that weekend was one showing an English football hooligan on the front, beer in one hand and brick in the other, with the slogan "England on Tour," and on the back, "England—Invasion of Germany, 1988."

The fans say that they have to "show" opposing countries. The ways in which they have "showed" them—from the mid-seventies through to the mid-eighties, in cities throughout Holland, France, Spain, Belgium, Denmark, Switzerland, and Luxembourg—would once have caused wars. At some games, hundreds have been injured, dozens arrested. Seats have been ripped up and hurled onto the pitch. Fans have urinated on opposing fans. They've rampaged through the streets, smashing windows, looting stores, and setting cars on fire. They've trashed ferries, trains, and coaches. And as they did all this, they often changed "war, war, war!"

They clearly hadn't read Konrad Lorenz's famous book *On Aggression,* which I remembered from my years as a psychology student—a stunning analysis of aggression and territoriality, with an unfortunate last chapter in which Lorenz proposed that games—and in particular, football matches—be used as a means of channeling and defusing nationalistic aggression. As I sat there in the basement morgue of Fortress Wapping filling notebook after notebook with the details of football violence, it seemed as though England was exacting a peculiar revenge on Lorenz's pet theory.

At Heysel Stadium, where the retaining wall gave way, some of the English fans wore swastika armbands. In London's Chelsea Stadium, you can see Nazi salutes being given from the terraces. The National Front, England's neo-Nazi organization, sees football matches as perfect recruiting grounds, and a Young National Front magazine, *Bulldog,* published in the early eighties, became a football hooligan's bible when it began a "League of Louts," in which rival fans vied in retailing their exploits.

The police responded to all this by going underground, using classic infiltration techniques. From 1985 on, they uncovered a half dozen fan gangs, including the Lunatic Fringe of Derby County, the Gooners of Arsenal, and the Yiddos of Tottenham Hotspur.

Yes, the Yiddos. A name adopted in bravado by a bunch of

neo-Nazi thugs. There's not a Jew among them, but the Tottenham Hotspur stadium is close to Stamford Hill, where most of London's Orthodox Jews live, and the club's owner is Jewish. Opposing teams call them the Yids, and opposing fans chant "We hate the Yids" with great relish throughout a game.

Hardly anyone in England, even most Jews, thinks this particularly worthy of comment. "It's just a nickname," they say, "there's nothing behind it." Not even when the National Front recruits at football matches? When the swastika is seen on the terraces? When you can hear chants like "Kill the Yids"? It doesn't really mean anything, I was told. It's not worth the trouble of making a fuss. You shouldn't even mention it, really.

Among the gangs arrested in toto were Birmingham City's Zulu Warriors, who gave their version of a Zulu chant as they charged their victims and rampaged through shopping centers as well as football grounds. Thirty-six were arrested. Their business card read "Zapped by a Zulu."

Then there were the Chelsea Head-Hunters, arrested in 1987. They had crossbows and rifles in their arsenal, as well as the more conventional spiked maces and machetes. "You have been nominated and dealt with by the Chelsea Head-Hunters," said their card.

But the gang that attracted the most attention was the Inter-City Firm—West Ham supporters whose arsenal included Bren guns and spiked balls and chains. They traveled by rapid Inter-City train to away games, usually first class. They were the largest of the gangs, with one hundred and forty-five members, the majority of them in regular jobs—a fact which gave pause to those who maintained that football hooliganism was solely the result of unemployment. Among their ranks were a bank manager, building contractors, manufacturers, importers, solicitors' clerks, an insurance underwriter, and eight British Army soldiers, one of them a sergeant.

Their business card went for a classily understated tone: "You have been visited by the ICF."

Spiked balls and chains? Studded maces? Crossbows? Just the list of weapons reads like something out of *A Clockwork Orange* or *Mad Max*—bleakly futuristic movies come to life on the football turf of England today. The anarchic gangs, the medieval weaponry, the surrealism of the embossed business cards, the random violence at little or no provocation, the primitive tribalism. . . . This is a new kind of England, ready to shatter old myths at the least provocation. Anglophiles beware.

PETE and Dennis and Mike are not pleased. The score is 2–1 in favor of Manchester, and there are only five minutes left to play. A sullen resentment is building behind me, mutterings of "We'll get yer, yer bunch of bleeding wankers." (The word *wanker* does not appear in the *O.E.D.,* though its Biblical counterpart, *onanist,* does.)

The P.A. system crackles to life. "We request visiting supporters to wait five minutes after the game. At that time, you will be escorted safely off the grounds."

"What happens then?" I ask.

"You'll see," Pete says.

They're going wild on the Manchester terrace, jumping and screaming and singing and chanting, waving banners and fists. The police are in a nearly solid ring around the pitch now, facing out towards the crowd. More have moved in at the top of the Manchester terrace, and to the sides.

They're determined not to have trouble this week. The week before, at this same stadium, Arsenal had played Millwall. There'd been forty-two thousand packed in then, though it's hard to see where; the stadium seems full to capacity right now, with thirty-five thousand. When trouble started, the police charged the crowd. Forty-one fans were arrested, seventy-three were thrown out of the grounds, and two neighborhood pubs were trashed. Both fans and police were injured. That happened with only five hundred police on hand. There are more today.

When the police really expect trouble, you can get up to one thousand men on duty at a game. It's expensive. The year before, police presence at games had cost twenty million pounds just in overtime salaries, not including investment in closed-circuit television systems inside the grounds, video cameras outside, body scanners, metal detector gates in some stadiums, and extra fencing. On a regular Saturday, when there are only a couple of "flash point" games being played, there are four thousand five hundred men on duty at the games, at a cost of over one pound per supporter. If the luck of the draw indicates more flash points—games between clubs whose supporters have bad records for hooliganism—the numbers and the cost of policing rise accordingly. And no matter how many police there are, they can only guard in the stadium and around it. They can't stop incidents like the one in Glasgow where a minibus full of Celtics supporters drove by mistake through a neighborhood stronghold of archrival Rangers fans. A hail of stones hit the bus; one Celtics fan was stoned to death.

Since a solid triple line of police now blocks all possible exits from the Manchester terrace, the P.A. request is in fact an order. It's hard to tell if the Manchester fans are being protected or imprisoned.

The rest of us file out slowly through the narrow corridors of the antiquated stadium. It's dark already—the last half hour of the game was played under floodlights. Out in the open, exits from the home stands and terrace lead toward a major gate to the street, underneath the steeply stepped concrete structure of the main Arsenal terrace.

"Don't go too far to the right," says Hugh. "You don't want to get under the terrace."

I look up where he's pointing, and see the lights glinting on three streams of urine arching high in the air.

The force of the crowd carries us on. Pete and his mates have been carried off in another direction. I see a six-year-old clinging to his father's hand, staring up wide-eyed in anxiety at the press of people around him. I feel like spreading my arms wide to give him space, but I can't. There *is* no space.

Out in the street, I take a deep breath. It's nighttime, but there seems to be an extraordinary amount of light. And noise. It gets louder and louder, bouncing back and forth in the narrow street between the rows of houses. Then it takes shape: a helicopter, methodically flying low over the streets lining the stadium, with a strong searchlight picking out every detail as it goes.

I flinch as the light comes towards me. I want to turn away as it sweeps over me. It makes me feel guilty, as though I've done something that needs strong light shed on it.

And now I can see for the first time just how many police are out here. Hundreds of them on foot, and dozens of mounted riot police. The horses are huge—far larger than New York City police horses. And everywhere I look, police dogs—big Alsatian attack dogs sitting quietly, ready for command.

The police are moving everyone towards the Underground train station as quickly as they can. They've blocked some streets, and they look like they know what they're doing. I hang back and spot a likely policeman in the middle of the road, listening to his two-way radio.

"Excuse me officer," I say. Always a good beginning with an English constable, who is invariably charmed by the very idea of being called "officer."

He smiles. "You're not from here, are you?"

I stick to my quasi-American identity. "No, I'm from New York, and I was wondering what's happening here. It all looks very impressive."

Between messages into his radio he explains the operation to me. It is indeed very impressive. In fact it's a full paramilitary operation, carried out in tandem by the Metropolitan Police Force and the Transport Police.

The plan calls for complete physical separation of Arsenal and Manchester fans. They'll be taken into the Underground station from different sides, on alternate trains—one for Arsenal, one for Manchester, one for Arsenal, and so on. The police control the station entrance, and now they're moving everyone in sight onto the pavement, behind a solid line of police men, police dogs, and police horses. The road itself soon belongs entirely to the police.

The helicopter circles, flying low, and the searchlight swings over us. Above, on the roofs, the video cameras record faces. It's eerily quiet. Thirty-five thousand fans who've spent the last two hours shouting and booing, cheering and singing, have gone completely silent. The only sounds to be heard are the throb of the helicopter, the clopping of horses' hooves, and the crackle of police radios. And one other sound, a subdued undertone to the more obvious ones: the muffled shuffling of feet moving slowly along the pavement.

I look for Pete and Dennis and Mike, but it's hard to tell anyone apart under these circumstances. Everyone looks the same: hunched shoulders, shadowy faces, cowed and dispirited.

"I'm so ashamed you should see football this way," says the policeman. "They're morons, the lot of them—complete morons. They say you have to go to South America to see good football nowadays. It seems they really know about crowd control there."

Over on the other side of the station, another long line of shadowy gray faces appears. The Manchester United fans have been released from their terrace, taken out the back entrance, then shepherded the long way around the block to approach the station behind the triple police barrier. None of them are singing anymore.

The Transport Police report that a train's come through and taken the Arsenal fans on the platform. The station is clear. Manchester fans file in, while Arsenal fans wait in sullen silence. The helicopter continues its search. The horses stomp as they circle in the street. The radios crackle.

"They don't even know what football is," says the policeman. "They only know violence. I remember coming to games with my dad, and it was a joy. I mean, it was part of being a kid, you know? But I wouldn't bring my son to a game now. If he wants to see football, he has to watch it on the television. That's what these morons have done to football. They've taken it away from those of us who really love the game."

A train comes in and loads up with Manchester fans, the Transport Police search the station and make sure it's clear, then more Arsenal fans are allowed on in. It's a model exercise in riot control. No arrests, no violence. Just the dispiriting sight of hunched people shuffling forward under a searchlight, watched by hundreds of police. Within forty-five minutes of the end of the game, there's not a football fan in sight.

SWEET MEMORIES

DISILLUSIONING though England may be to those with fond images of justice and fairness, it still provides the small grace notes of everyday life that take me unawares, and that I miss in New York City: the smell of new-mown grass on a sunny afternoon, the sound of church bells on a Sunday morning, the tastes of an English childhood . . .

A pause, then, for sweet memories. A pause, in fact, in praise of English foods. Yes, praise.

I confess I can hardly claim objectivity in the matter. The stomach is the last part of the anatomy to part ways with its native country. The head leaves first, and then the heart, but there remains an atavistic sense of belonging, literally in the gut.

A simple trip to the supermarket can turn me into a loose cannon of nostalgia. I come back to Hugh and Rosie's house laden down with grocery bags. They stare, dumbfounded, as I unload the bags, item by item, onto the kitchen counter. Since I often stay with them when I'm in London, they've seen me go through this ritual many times before, but still they can't disguise a bemused astonishment. There seems to be something about an adult longing for childhood foods that remains peculiarly amusing and disturbing at the same time, rather like a child dressing up in adult's clothes.

I shrug as I unload my cache of childhood. It includes cream buns—bland confectioner's dough split open down the middle, stuffed with confectioner's cream and a dollop of raspberry jam, and sprinkled with confectioner's sugar. A big bag of Maltesers—chocolate-covered balls of malt which melt in your mouth leaving a sticky solidified lump. Clotted cream, which I rip open and dig into with a spoon, delighting in the real fresh cream unknown to any American who lives more than half a mile from a farm. Malt extract—the thick, sweet, syrupy concoction that we were fed by the National Health in the late forties and fifties: vitamins for the children. Polo mints—"The Mint with a Hole"—the ones I can still never keep whole in my mouth, all the way to melting, without cracking them between my teeth. Rowntree's fruit gums, which the manufacturers used to promote with contests to see who could make a fruit gum last longest; the record, I seem to remember, was something like forty-five minutes.

I never eat all of this. Who could? One taste of each item is generally enough; my eyes are far larger than my stomach. I grab for everything as though making up for the years of rationing after World War Two.

I don't even remember exactly how old I was the day they withdrew rationing on sugar and candies. I do remember my mother taking me into the candy store and telling me I could have anything I wanted. Anything at all. And I remember looking around the store, my eyes trying to take in the vast assortment of sweets—licorice allsorts and aniseed balls and fruit gums and Maltesers and sherbet dabs and Mars Bars and chewy mints and Crunchies and licorice comfits and dolly mixture and pastilles and candied almonds and dark toffees and light toffees and coconut bars and barley sugar and hard mints and candied fudge and boiled sweets and fruity chews. . . . All in big glass jars with screw tops, each one with its lavender-bordered label and the name and price carefully inscribed in ornate confectioner's script.

"Come on," said my mother. "Take whatever you want. No more coupons." And the woman behind the counter smiled like a beneficent angel of childhood.

But I couldn't. I was too used to going in there once a week and asking for a farthing's worth of aniseed balls. You got eight for a farthing, and you could make an aniseed ball last for an hour if you were careful and took it out of your mouth every now and again to examine the change in color from deep purplish red to pure white as you sucked it down to its core. And so, with that whole wonderful range of sugared delights at my command, I reached up over the counter—I must have been four or five if I needed to reach up—and said:

"Eight aniseed balls please."

But now even the aniseed balls aren't as I remember them. They seem smaller, for a start. And now that I am an adult, I don't take them out of my mouth to examine them every few minutes. That was as much a part of the pleasure as the taste. Besides, now they cost two pence each. Which equals four old pence. And that was sixteen farthings. Which means that the cost of a single aniseed ball has increased one-hundred-and-twenty-eight-fold since I was five.

I measure inflation in aniseed balls.

Do all emigrants go through this when they return to visit their country of birth? Do they all fill up their stomachs on childhood foods as though they've been deprived for years of some basic nurture? And then wonder, the next day, why they feel somewhat sick?

ROBERTSON'S jams were also part of my childhood, part of the food that had comforted me as I was growing up. That's why the golliwogs were so friendly, why it was so easy to pay no attention. What could possibly be bad about jams? They were a literal incorporation of Englishness.

Jam was one of those English staples that crossed class barriers. Everybody ate jam, though the class showed in the manner of eating it. The upper class favored genteel dollops to the side of a plate of hot buttered toast, while the working class took it straight out of the jam jar, spreading it as thick as the budget would allow onto sliced white bread with plenty of butter—or, if times were tight, margarine. Jam was a luxury addition to the basic "butty"—the bread-and-butter sandwich that was a staple item of a working-class diet in the fifties.

We never ate butties when I was a child. We were upper middle class, and in food, as in all else, the English maintain a definite tradition of class distinction. I never even knew butties existed until I went north to university at Manchester, where a whole new England was revealed to me. For two of my three years there, I shared an apartment with a friend on Lavender Grove, very near the university. It was a slum. At the end of the road, a mile down, was what the neighbors called "the rats' nest"—the main police station of Manchester. Half a mile to the east was Moss Lane East, known as the murder mile of England, with the highest rate of murders per year in the whole country. Next door was a brothel.

Food was not elegant in that part of Manchester. Food was what came cheap and filled your stomach. There were certain staples: baked beans on toast, for instance—easy to make (open the can of Heinz beans, heat, pour over toast) and comfortingly warming. Or bacon butties—a couple of strips of fried bacon between the slabs of buttered white bread. Or pork pies in the pub, pale rounds of damp pastry surrounding a tiny ball of pale pink ground substance, which included much filler and some pork—we took that on faith—made edible by liberally applying a certain thick brown bottled sauce unknown in upper-class homes. And of course, fish and chips.

We bought them late at night—the fish-and-chip shops stayed open to attract beery customers turned out of the pubs at the eleven o'clock closing time—and then walked home watching our breath cloud in the freezing air, clutching the newspaper cones with their hot, oily cargo of chips drenched in vinegar.

The vinegar was essential; it was the only way to make the chips remotely edible.

The chips—known in the States as French fries, though the

French would recoil in horror at the thought—were cut long and thick from old potatoes full of eyes and black spots. They were cooked slowly in huge vats of oil kept at a temperature just below boiling so that the chips emerged soft and soggy, with the oil worked all the way through each long thick piece.

They were threepence or fourpence a portion, I don't remember which, and we'd lift them up, one by one, high above our upturned faces, watching them bend limply, and then feed them into our mouths. We were young and healthy and hungry, and nothing could satisfy those nighttime hungers like good old-fashioned chips.

We never ate the fish. Doused in batter, then deep-fried alongside the chips, it came out as a tasteless white filling inside a thick layer of half-cooked dough. Besides, it was more expensive than just a portion of chips.

Of course, for us it was an adventure. Middle-class kids living temporarily on a working-class level, on subsistence government grants, working summers and Christmas vacations to supplement those grants or pay for a vacation, we could afford to make an experience of it. We knew we didn't have to live that way for the rest of our lives. We could always go home and eat well. We were tourists in the working-class world.

And everywhere we went in that world, we were offered that working-class English classic—a nice cuppa tea.

A nice cuppa tea is a synonym for comfort. Homely comfort, not the posh drawing-room kind. At its most bracing, it used to come canteen style, milk and sugar already added, in blue and white striped mugs. Always those same mugs, the stripes a half-inch thick and the brew "strong enough to stand your spoon in."

That's the way it came on the trains, in roadside cafes, and in workers' canteens.

"Want a cuppa tea, luv?" the tea man would say with a nod and a wink as he pulled open the sliding door that led onto the corridor. British Rail tea men always winked. The trick was to stop them squeezing your knee as they handed you the mug. And if you asked for tea without sugar, you'd get another wink and a leer: "Sweet enough already, then?"

"Time for a cuppa," the truck driver would say as we drove south from Manchester to London. I was hitchhiking, on my way to see my boyfriend, and we'd pull into a roadside cafe and the trucker would treat an impoverished student to a huge English breakfast with everything fried—eggs and bacon and tomatoes and sausages—and bread-and-butter sandwiches to go with them and mop up all the juices, and of course tea, and steam on the windows, and the friendly hum of talk.

And at the post office, freezing from the long walk in the pre-dawn dark to start the sorting for my Christmas mail route, a student job just for the holiday season, I'd be greeted with "Here we go, then, a nice cuppa tea, something to thaw your bones out." And I'd wrap my hands around the mug to thaw out my fingers, and sip slowly to thaw out my insides, and carry the tea to the stack of pigeonholes where I'd linger over the sorting before venturing out into the cold again to deliver the day's bounty of Christmas greetings.

I drank tea without sugar then, a remnant from those postwar days of strict sugar rationing in which I grew up, but I took the pre-sugared tea gratefully. It was the taste of England, of a huge real country out there, a country I could visit and be in for a while but never really live in. Not with my BBC accent, not with my education. It was a world far removed from upper-class daintily glazed bone china, from worrying about liquid slopped into the saucer or how to balance the saucer on genteelly crossed knees or finding a comfortable position for the little finger without sticking it out in absurd affectation. It was a vacation from having to behave according to my class.

Those blue and white striped mugs are long gone now. I haven't seen one in well over twenty years. The British Rail tea man doesn't exist any more, and neither do those separate compartments. The modern trains have open carriages, and there's no longer a corridor to push a tea trolley along, nor any of those odd situations once so beloved of British moviemakers, where six strangers sit together in a closed compartment, covertly eyeing each other from behind newspapers and half-closed eyes. And the truckers' cafes have disappeared too, replaced by the motorway cafeteria chains, which favor styrofoam cups over blue and white mugs, and lukewarm tea-bagged water over the carefully brewed pot.

THE tea bag is fast and convenient. A very American idea. But if you were to suggest to the English that their tea habits were becoming Americanized, they'd be shocked. And they'd be even more shocked if you pointed out that they were drinking a stimulant.

That's not for us, they'd say, that's for them Yanks. They drink coffee on the run, while we sit down to our tea. You may "grab a coffee," but you never grab a cuppa tea; you settle down to it, make yourself comfy, relax. Coffee's fast, tea's solid. Coffee hypes you up, tea settles you down. And if the physiologists tell you otherwise, then they're obviously American physiologists.

It's two hundred years since three hundred chests of prime East India Company tea were thrown overboard in Boston harbor, and other consignments left to rot on the wharves in Charleston and sent back untouched from Philadelphia and New York. The Boston Tea Party was perfectly calculated as a rejection of the Old World, of England's dominion, of kings, queens, and Empire. Wise Sam Adams drowned the tea instead of downing it, arousing such indignation in England that the powers that be were goaded into over-reaction.

But now, two centuries later, the transatlantic balance of power has shifted, and the former colonies are exacting a strange revenge. The English can be seen using tea bags, drinking Coca-Cola, even brewing coffee first thing in the morning. But the ultimate triumph of American foods was the ouster of what once seemed the unbreachable tradition of fish and chips.

There is, of course, no reason to assume that England would be any more resistant to the fast-food invasion than the rest of the world, even though the very idea would have been inconceivable when I was a child. The English were still hyper-suspicious of all things foreign then, and most of all, of foreign foods. But to replace one kind of bad food with another is a fairly simple proposition for a sophisticated marketer, especially in a country whose former resistance to all things American is waning as fast as the memories of its own imperial greatness.

At first it seemed a sacrilege of sorts. A McDonald's behind lead-paned bow windows on a quaint little cobbled high street? Someone's idea of a joke, perhaps. But you can see the horribly familiar signs all over England now, even unto the hallowed high-rent hills of Hampstead and Highgate. McDonald's, Kentucky Fried Chicken, Burger King—as England's Americaphilia has grown, so have the fast-food outlets, pushing out the old fish-and-chip shops.

The American invaders made one basic miscalculation, however. They forgot to factor in England's class system, which applies as much to food as it does to everything else. If fish and chips were lower-class, so too, inevitably, were their replacements. The upper classes raised their noses high, wrinkled them in disgust, and went as far as they could in the other direction—into a renaissance of traditional English food.

When English cooking is done well, it's hard to imagine why anyone ever thought it bad. Just the thought of a perfectly roasted beef, rare in the center and crisp on the outside, served with braised turnips and a light, moist Yorkshire pudding, is enough to make the mouth water. It's an art, this cuisine, as much an art as Italian or French. It was long lost, and now it's returning.

You can find it on the menus of country inns and restaurants in Berkshire, Wiltshire, Hertfordshire, Oxfordshire—throughout the southern counties. If you can find them, that is. They're often so small and out-of-the-way that you need a detailed map, but educated diners now drive up to two hours out of London along verdant summer back roads to sit down to traditional English delights: the treasures of the game warden—venison and pheasant, partridge and wild duck, the most delicate salmon—followed by creamy English desserts: not the heavy cakes so loved of Americans, and no chocolate, but pure cream and fruit combined into syllabubs and gooseberry fools, or the simple pleasure of meringues and fresh-picked raspberries.

It's good food, it's expensive, and it's upper-class. Where lower-class food is being invaded by America, upper-class food is going Ur-English. It could be seen, perhaps, as an attempt to fulfill Margaret Thatcher's dictum of putting the "great" back in Great Britain, except that the upper class can barely tolerate Thatcher. To them, she has committed the greatest sin of all: She is middle-class.

PANDORA'S BOX

MONEY used to be very lower-class. One simply didn't mention it. It betrayed bad breeding to do so. It spoke of "trade," a word pronounced with that upper-class sneer reserved solely for the tiresome middle classes. Those who dealt openly with money, such as bookies, were considered incredibly vulgar, given to wearing loud plaid jackets very much like American ones.

The upper classes dealt with money, to be sure, and plenty of it, but that was in the refined atmosphere of the Stock Exchange or Lloyd's, where there was no actual contact between flesh and the green stuff. The English attitude to money was that of a fastidious matron faced with the incontrovertible need to use a public toilet: "But you never know what's touched it before."

Only the closed oak and mahogany doors of gentlemen's clubs and attorney's consulting rooms could contain the smell of it. It was one of those things that one couldn't get along without, but that one preferred to ignore if at all possible. It was rather like Victorian sex.

All of which is why Caryl Churchill's play *Serious Money* was such a hit in England.

Set in the City of London post Big Bang, it was similar to the movie *Wall Street* in taking Ivan Boesky's paean to greed as its theme. Written in dispiriting doggerel verse, with dogmatic ideology served up like lashings of bright red canned spaghetti sauce, it seemed an uncertain cross between street theater and college revue. But from its opening in 1987, the boys and girls from the City turned out en masse for it, the prospect of seeing themselves lampooned on stage apparently irresistible.

Picture one intermission, early in the play's West End run, with a dozen or so Sloane-Ranger types—young upper-class chinless wonders—gathered in a circle in the tiny foyer to share a couple of bottles of "poo," their nursery nickname for champagne. The play had clearly worked some magic on them. They were chanting out one of its songs—basically a string of four-letter words capped by the dirtiest word of all: money. The women giggled and tossed their hair. They gave little darting glances over their shoulders to see who was watching, eyes gleaming with that "oh-look-how-daring-we-are" thrill. The men held their ground, daring each other to continue by staring into each other's eyes. They waved their glasses and spilled their champagne as the chant gathered speed and intensity. Oh, the excitement! They'd never seen money so openly talked about in public before, never heard it so nakedly yearned for. The flush on the women's faces and the machismo triumph in their escorts' eyes spoke it clearly: Caryl Churchill had opened a Pandora's box. Money was exciting, a sexual turn-on. Money was the latest four-letter word, the revolution had happened, and now they could say it, sing it, chant it, and get the same frisson of guilty, rebellious excitement as a convent schoolgirl saying "fuck" for the first time.

The play pandered to both sides of the coin: It condemned and glorified greed at the same time, satisfying the shards of conscience while whetting the appetite for more. This made it the perfect play for the time.

The Big Bang of October 1986 had liberated the antiquated and restrictive rules of the Stock Exchange, putting London in line with Tokyo and New York in the international free-trading market. Suddenly, the City was stripped of its mask of gentility, and the naked greed of Wall Street came surging onto center stage.

The Stock Exchange had been a closed gentlemen's shop; now it was suddenly a brightly lit supermarket. Quick-thinking working-class lads began to make fortunes in commissions on the trading floors. "Gorblimey brokers," they called them, or "barrow-boy brokers"—lads who'd played back-room roles before, and who now stepped into the limelight, making money for themselves instead of for their superiors. And, since they knew no better, spending it in splendidly un-English ostentation.

The naked greed of Wall Street unmasked the hidden greed of City gentility. Within a few months of the Big Bang, all the symptoms were in full bloom—Porsches, cocaine, insider trading, the lot. Champagne replaced beer as the only drink that mattered. The stuff bubbled, frothed, overflowed all around the City. Bars served nothing but bubbly as rock-music videos blared above the counter and the Tokyo stock prices flashed by on the bottom of the screen, the perfect subscript to Madonna's stylish tackiness. Blankley's, right by Lloyd's in the newly gentrified Leadenhall Market, sold only three items: champagne, caviar, and cigars.

Oh, what fun! Not just to be rich, but to show it! Discretion had been rather boring all those years, one had to admit. And inconvenient too. It was one thing to realize that a twenty-year-old Jaguar was far more stylish than a brand-new one, but quite another to maintain it. And though a dilapidated country mansion was far more respectable than a fully renovated one, my dear, one did suffer from the draughts, you know.

Inconspicuous consumption was definitely passé. The pie had gone public, and everyone wanted a piece of it. Which meant that everyone was talking about money. Big money.

Still a captive of the older English attitude to the stuff, I was shocked. Since I had grown up Jewish in England, and since the Shylock stereotype of Jewish avarice was so strong, I'd developed a fine disregard for money, taking my cue from the upper-class disdain for it. It took me years to realize that such an attitude is fine only if you have lots of money to begin with, which I didn't.

Now I was astonished by the ease with which new acquaintances regaled me with tales of wealth. Without even asking, I knew how much their homes had appreciated in value over the last year, how they'd done on the stock market, how much a case of port they'd laid away ten years before was worth now, how much they sold their grandmother's paintings for at auction. I wouldn't have asked, of course—I couldn't have done that. One never, but never, used to ask about money in England. But *they* asked, stunning me with the directness of their questions, so un-English, so . . . American. How much had I paid for my apartment in Manhattan? What did one need a year to live there? Didn't I want to buy a summer place in Ibiza?

Deprived for so long of the delights of greed—the flamboyant demonstrativeness of money's power, the gleaming vulgarity of its results—the English were discovering the heady delights of letting it show. All the acquisitiveness repressed over forty years of welfare-state socialism was spurting out like froth from a bottle of champagne. Perhaps as a result of all the cocaine, money had suddenly lost its smell and England came rearing out of the gate, racing ahead into an era of rampant capitalism.

••**I** want a capital-earning democracy," declared Margaret Thatcher in 1983. "Every man and woman a capitalist. Housing is the start. . . . Every man a capitalist, and every man a property owner."

And there was light. Thirty years ago, one-third of all Britons owned their own homes. Today, it's two-thirds. And those homes have shot up in value. In the late eighties, houses were gaining by sixty percent a year in certain areas of central England, with an average of sixteen percent throughout the country and thirty percent for anywhere within an hour-and-a-half's drive of London. True, the market remained completely depressed in Northern Ireland and places like Liverpool, but country cottages in the Lake District, just an hour's drive north of Liverpool and five hours from London, fetched London prices as weekend and vacation homes. Property prices in the elite areas of London—Knightsbridge, Belgravia, Mayfair—made Fifth Avenue look like a steal. And New Yorkers proud of their summer weekend homes in the Hamptons stared in astonishment as Londoners flew off for weekends to their romantic villas in Spain.

The Thatcher government began a policy of selling off council houses to their tenants. Each home purchased was a vote purchased for the Conservatives, known historically as the Tories. While the inner-city public-housing developments remained ghettos of drugs, violence, desolate walkways, filthy stairwells, and broken-down elevators—virtual prisons of the unemployed—more and more people elsewhere attained the heights of the middle class. "Basically," said one member of Parliament, "Thatcher's hijacked the Tory party from the landowners and given it to the real-estate agents."

Margaret Thatcher is a dilemma for any self-respecting Anglophobe such as myself. She's systematically pulling apart everything I ever thought good about England—the health system, the educational system, the welfare state—an England in which, no matter how bad things were, everyone had the basic assurance of shelter and food and health care, of a decent education and a decent meal. A decent England. A kinder, gentler England. But then she's also pulling apart many of the things I ever thought bad about England—prime among them, the class system.

"I want to get totally rid of class distinction," she declared in 1985. "As someone put it in one of the papers this morning: Marks & Spencer have triumphed over Marx and Engels."

The trouble is, I'm not at all sure that Marks & Spencer is an improvement over Marx and Engels.

"England is a nation of shopkeepers," jibed Napoleon two hundred years ago. "And that," Margaret Thatcher seems to be saying, "is what made us great." The woman is haunted by greatness. She raises high the flag of a cliché-ridden provincial England, as in her campaign slogan of 1983, "Let's put the 'great' back in Great Britain." Britain is the word for her, not England, not because she cares about Scotland or Wales or Northern Ireland—all her policies, in fact, show she doesn't—but because her Britain, the Britain of her father's house, was great, grand, and imperial. Somewhere beneath that middle-class exterior beats an imperial heart. If she could, Margaret Thatcher would resurrect the Empire.

If I see her in an ideal setting, it's a small colonial outpost in India, before 1948 and all those ungrateful excesses by which the Indian subcontinent claimed its independence and rejected the benevolence of British imperialism. She'd be head of the outpost, of course, the perfect colonial civil servant, insisting on order and cleanliness, on the natives not stealing and the whites not drinking too much. Her little printed dresses with sensible hemlines and floppy bows at the neck would be perfectly in place as she opened the polo tourney or the cricket match, standing awkwardly at the microphone, not a hair out of place, not a bead of sweat on her upper lip as those around her fainted and swooned in the tropical heat. Her hectoring manner would be perfect for addressing the natives, who everyone knows have to be talked to loudly and simply or they'll just pretend they don't understand.

It's easy enough to make fun of her this way. The problem is that in doing so, I confuse style and content. In the context of England, it's hard not to. Thatcher's manner, style, and dress all offend me as much as her policies. In that, I am as guilty of snobbery as the worst of the intellectual snobs who oppose her. Who loathe her, in fact. With a venom quite extraordinary by English standards.

Here, for example, is Jonathan Miller, the renaissance man of arts and science—doctor, writer, satirist, opera director— known for his cool, wry sophistication, responding to a reporter's question on why the vast majority of the intellectual and cultural establishment is so deeply hostile to Thatcher: "Isn't the reason self-evident? It's the same as why the bulk of the human race is hostile to typhoid." Besides, he added, "I can't stand her odious suburban gentility and sentimental, saccharine patriotism, catering to the worst elements of commuter idiocy."

This isn't even intellectual snobbery. This is the old, familiar class snobbery, the Oxbridge disdain of "trade," the urban connoisseur in his carefully renovated town house so smugly superior to the suburban commuter in his brand-new fake Gothic home.

The reporter then tried Lady Warnock, mistress of Cambridge's top women's college, Girton, who cited Thatcher's tone of derision and anger when speaking about the universities. Fair enough, but she then added that even if that were to change, the way Thatcher shouted people down epitomized the worst of the lower middle class. There's her patronizing, elocution-lesson voice, said Lady Warnock, like that of a primary-school headmistress losing patience with the children. And then Thatcher's neat, well-groomed clothes and hair were "packaged together in a way that's not exactly vulgar, just *low.*"

Lady Warnock, of course, would never dream of accusing the Queen of being "low," even though Margaret Thatcher has evidently taken the Queen for her model, ghastly handbags, out-of-date hats, tightly controlled hairstyle and all. In fact, since Thatcher came to power in 1979, she and the Queen have done a sort of Dorian Gray number: While the Queen has become frumpier by the day, Thatcher has become positively daring with the blusher and eyeliner.

In pique, perhaps, at being outdone as England's leading lady, the Queen is said to loathe Thatcher, but for the very best of upper-class reasons: The woman is an arriviste, a grocer's daughter with an absurdly phony upper-class accent (very similar to the Queen's, incidentally, though the Queen always sounds as if she's just getting a cold, and Margaret Thatcher seems as invulnerable to colds as she is to criticism). It's the pretentiousness that irks the upper classes, who can't forgive the fact that Thatcher is the product of the utmost in middle-class provincialism—the small town of Grantham (population 25,000), two hours and a whole world north of London.

Thatcher senior was also a Methodist lay preacher—Methodist! Preacher! My dear, how vulgar!—and his daughter says she went to church several times every Sunday (though in uncharacteristic carelessness the number of times changes from interview to interview—sometimes four, sometimes two or three). By her own account, her childhood was unremittingly joyless. Pathetically so.

"I was brought up very, very seriously," she's said. "I was a very serious child and we were not allowed to go out to much entertainment. Going out to a film was a very big treat. . . . I don't think I ever went to a dance until I was at university. Dancing was frowned upon by my parents. Dancing was forbidden. I was allowed to learn ballet and eurhythmics because that was cultural, but everything always had to have some cultural content."

Poor Maggie, feeding the critics who accuse her of not being "amusing," as though British intellectual snobs would prefer the genial good-times of a Ronald Reagan. She certainly doesn't know how. When she tries to be charming, she comes on as gushy instead. Her humor comes out mean and cutting, like her taunting of liberal critics as "moaning minnies" or "the chattering classes." Her brittle, aggressive style has earned her the epithets of "strident" and "fishwife." And far from evading the suburban housewife image, she actually plays on it, to the point of urging the English, the day after her last election, to improve their manners, forswear litter and graffiti, and "keep your own house nice and clean as a bright new pin."

"No style," is the consensus. Absolutely no style. Even her anti-Establishment populism is a fake. A grocer's daughter, yes, but that grocer was the mayor of Grantham, chairman of the board of governors of the local grammar school, and host to Conservative ministers when they came to town. While fifteen-year-old shop girls weighed out sugar in the store downstairs, Margaret studied upstairs for Oxbridge. As Robert Chessyre of *The Observer* put it, "the spoon in the mouth had been at the very least silver-plated."

That, of course, is the ultimate mistake—the tacky tawdriness of silver plate. The ultimate middle-classness of it. That and her penny-wise-pound-foolish philosophy, the way she brought all the old saws of the provincial high street into government.

The last thing anyone could have expected from such a woman is that she be a radical. But that she is. Not only is she the longest-serving prime minister of this century, she's also the first to adopt a truly radical policy—the first to challenge, and to set about changing, the whole way England runs. The old money of the Tory party loathes her in equal measure to the liberal intellectuals, and for good reason. She's completely outside the old gentlemen's club system of the Tory party. In fact she led a major revolution inside the party, ending the dominance of the traditional Tories—mainly landed gentry with public-school backgrounds—and opening it up to those who, like herself, wanted to "better themselves." Like a gate-crasher who becomes the life and soul of the party, she's taken over.

Don't be deceived, then, by all that talk about style. The real source of the venom is this threat to the whole system of privilege. Thatcher is the middle-class leader par excellence, and she's out to make the whole of England into her own image. Which means she's as much at war with the upper class as with the working class.

This kind of warfare suits her. She proudly acknowledges that she thrives on antagonism. The same cannot be said of the Labour opposition, which has played a major role in helping her stay in power. Through the seventies and the early eighties, the left wing of Labour went through an absurdly self-destructive radicalization. The dogmatic theatrics of the Marxist section pulled the Labour party apart, deepening the economic woes of those cities like Liverpool where they controlled the councils and offering Thatcher the opportunity to break the power of the unions by taking a determined stand against their absolutism. So threatened was the burgeoning middle class with the prospect of out-and-out class war that liberalism was abandoned and Thatcher could present herself as the refuge against anarchy.

And the key to it all was money. Margaret Thatcher appreciates money. She knows its power. She talks openly of it, and you can sense her Methodist upbringing in the way she talks. The woman who once called for "a crusade to stop the onward march of socialism once and for all," also stated that "Pennies do not come from heaven; they have to be earned here on earth." And in one of her best-remembered bons mots: "No one would have remembered the Good Samaritan if he'd only had good intentions; he had money as well."

Yes, the woman is positively shameless about money. She's like one of those horribly efficient staff nurses or headmistresses, all starch and brisk common sense, who won't tolerate any nonsense from those in her charge and insists on calling a spade a spade: "There's no need to be ashamed—they're all natural functions, you know."

And what was more natural than that the middle class should begin to indulge in formerly upper-class pastimes, such as owning shares? Since Thatcher came to power, English shareholders have quadrupled to one out of every five voters. As more and more nationalized industries have been privatized, middle-class punters have leaped on the opportunity to buy telephone, airline, and automobile shares at day-of-issue prices, and sat back to enjoy the particular pleasure of watching unearned income accrue.

For them she's "our Maggie"—a term of endearment as insulting in its way as "that bloody woman," since nobody, but nobody, would ever have dreamed of calling Churchill "our Winnie." It's an almost desperate attempt to make her lovable, but the fact is, she's a hard woman to love. She makes do with respect instead. And every time someone buys their own house, or invests in shares, Margaret Thatcher gains another vote in the next elections.

She's become the champion of the middle class. And by making the middle class wealthier, she expands her power base year by year. There are four times as many millionaires in England as when she came to power; suddenly wealth has become possible. The fact that there are also nearly three times as many unemployed is one of those things that's easy to ignore unless you happen to be unemployed yourself.

The middle class have been waiting for someone like her, reassuringly Tory down to the soles of her low-heeled pumps. This isn't really war on the class system; she's a right-wing radical, not a class warfare warrior. It's an attempt to create an England where the terms of class are changed. In Thatcher's ideal England, class won't disappear, it will be determined differently. In her England, entrepreneurs and industrialists will be rewarded with knighthoods, no matter what their education or their accent. "Trade" will offer the glittering prizes, not inheritance. Money, not birth, will create the new nobility. It will be, in short, an American England.

IT'S doubtful if any American president spends even one minute thinking about England for every hour Margaret Thatcher spends thinking about America. "As you know," she told one reporter in 1987, "I am Ronald Reagan's greatest fan."

Even her rhetoric has become American. In a Conservative party political broadcast just before the 1987 elections, she painted her picture of the future: "Come with us, then, towards the next decade. Let us together set our sights on a Britain where three out of four families own their home, where owning shares is as common as owning a car, where families have a degree of independence their forefathers could only dream about. . . ." She spoke to rapturous applause. And why not? England never had political dreams before. Only America did. The dream even came replete with forefathers, a word never before used in the English political lexicon—an American word.

She's the first English prime minister ever to be accused of running her government like an American president and ever to have staged an American-type electoral campaign, with Saatchi & Saatchi, one of the world's top advertising companies, as her media consultants. As writer Angela Carter sourly noted just after the 1987 electoral victory, "Now we have all the disadvantages of America without any of the advantages."

Thatcher's advisors, known derisively as her "laughing boys," are not at all typical of the Conservative male animal. "There have been too many Jews, too many philanderers, too many advertising men and too many homosexuals in Mrs. Thatcher's club," wrote Germaine Greer in 1988. "She's unclubbable, and therein lies her true radicalism. The old guard has been removed from the center of power."

An old university friend of mine is one of the "laughing boys." Probably because we've spent most of the intervening time in separate countries, the friendship has lasted. Thatcher may not be amusing or charming, but she chooses men who are. Over dinner one night, I asked him about the north-south divide—the fact that the prosperous south of England is almost entirely pro-Thatcher, while the north, where unemployment is highest and people describe themselves as "disposable" in the eyes of the government, is almost solidly anti.

He shrugged. "It takes time, that's all," he said. "In the 1983 elections, England was pro-Thatcher up to Watford, just north of London. By 1987, it had reached the Midlands. The next elections, it'll reach the north of England."

And then he launched into an extraordinary tirade. People should be pleased at what she's doing, he said. She's making the real revolution. Many of the senior people close to Thatcher haven't been Oxbridge educated. In fact, they haven't been to university at all. "That's what's happening," he said. "We're finally displacing those high-falutin' bastards whose rich mummies and daddies got them into Oxbridge. We've had generations of 'being' whoever you are in England. Now we've got people *doing*. Who you are is not important to Margaret Thatcher—it's what you do that matters. Doing the job. Not people who sit back on their titles and look down on the rest of us, but people who get out there and get their hands dirty and create jobs and get things working again. We've taken the Tory party away from the old fogies of privilege and class. Those bastards have had it."

"The revenge of the middle class," I said.

He grinned. "And revenge is sweet," he said. "Sweet indeed."

I was surprised at the venom. Thatcher is capable of arousing it on both sides. This man is usually charming and fey. He always was, even when we knew each other in university, when we marched together in the Campaign for Nuclear Disarmament. But where I stayed liberal, he's swung way over to the right, to Margaret Thatcher's side. This amuses him. He teases me by reminding me of the old saw that whoever is not a socialist at twenty has no heart, and whoever is not a capitalist at forty has no sense.

It was raining and late at night by the time we left the restaurant. I was unlocking my car door when he called to me to wait and came dashing across the street, skipping between the headlights, to press something into my hand. "Just for you," he said breathlessly, kissed me good night, and skipped back across the street to his own car.

I looked down. In my hand was a Conservative party pennant on a plastic stick. He waved, grinning, as he drove off. I laughed, waved the pennant in return, and threw it in the nearest trash can. I had no intention of waving the flag for the woman who was destroying the welfare state.

IMMEDIATELY after her 1987 victory, Margaret Thatcher announced "a radical legislative plan" which amounted to a practical declaration of war on what for me was always the brightest star of the England I grew up in—the National Health Service.

It's true I have a vested interest. My father was a National Health doctor, a general practitioner who truly believed in the system, in the principle of free high-level health care for all. He was an old-style Liberal, who in a moment of political naiveté stood for the local town council and was elected, the only Liberal to be elected in something like fifty years, and certainly the only Irish Jew. Through no fault or desire of his own, his one vote held the balance of power between Tories and Labourites on the council. A born politician would have given his eyeteeth and a lot more to be in that situation.

I must have been about ten at the time, and you could say my political education started when he returned home from his first council meeting. He looked somewhat dazed. My mother asked how it had gone. He shook his head and sat down at the head of the table like a man who'd just discovered that his bank manager had embezzled all his savings.

"Politics," he said, "is completely amoral."

He served out his term, stubbornly voting his conscience on every issue and totally flummoxing the political system of the council, and never got involved in politics again.

That same conscience made him a National Health doctor from the system's inception in 1946 until his retirement a few years ago. He believed in the system and never even thought of private practice. The town of Reading, some forty miles west of London, has expanded to close to a quarter million people, but it's still hard to walk the town center with him without someone coming up to tell him that a baby he delivered twenty years ago has just gotten married. My childhood was punctuated by the phone ringing in the middle of the night, the sounds of my father hurriedly dressing and the door slamming as he went out into a cold winter's night to deal with an emergency, and whispered conversation an hour or two later when he climbed back into bed and my mother rolled over to ask what it had been.

"Dehydrated baby—had to send him to the hospital."

"Old lady panicking—just needed calming."

"Premature birth—a girl."

When he retired, there were so many cards from former patients that they covered the whole of the living-room floor. To my astonishment, he remembered them all.

So it was sad—sensible, but sad—when some years ago, needing open-heart surgery, he elected for a private hospital over a National Health Service one.

The surgeon who performed the surgery was the same one who would have performed it under the National Health. The difference was in the vital aftercare. Instead of the drab misery of a National Health ward, understaffed with underpaid nurses and undersupplied with basic medical necessities, he had the intensive care and attention of a private room in a small private hospital off Harley Street. Like everyone who can afford it in England, even he had finally abandoned the National Health.

In 1988, there were twice as many nurses working in private health care as four years before. Not because the wages are higher—they're on the same abysmal scale, with a staff nurse earning seven thousand three hundred pounds a year, gross, after eight years on the wards—but because physical working conditions, hours, medical supplies, and so on are far, far better. Meanwhile, whole National Health hospital wards are being shut down. Not for lack of patients—there are too many patients, and anyone with anything less than an absolute emergency operation can be postponed for months and even years at a time—but for lack of nursing staff and basic medical supplies.

Barmaids earn about one pound eighty an hour in England; many nurses moonlight as barmaids to eke out their earnings. Others take off for Kuwait or Oman or any other of the Persian Gulf states for a year or two, coming back with enough to buy a small apartment or to leave nursing altogether. The status of the National Health Service has decreased as more and more Indian and Pakistani doctors have come into it, replacing white doctors. Prejudice does its work, and white patients avoid Asian doctors if they can. Only the very best Asian doctors even think of private practice; most know they will never get a substantial base of white middle-class patients.

Worst of all, the National Health Service has been systematically underfunded by the Thatcher government, which encourages private health insurance for those who can afford it and sees the N.H.S. as the fallback system for those who can't. Private health insurance schemes have proliferated, shoring up the private health-care sector and undermining the public one. Now Thatcher wants only those who use the N.H.S. to pay for it in their taxes—only those, that is, who cannot afford the private option. It's a step coldly calculated to impoverish the whole service even more. Eventually, the N.H.S. will become an emergency service for the poor, the old, and the catastrophically ill; and what seemed to me the best of England—the guarantee of free, high-level health care for all—will become as impossibly absurd a concept as it is in the United States.

Early in 1988, National Health Service nurses called a one-day strike. In an attempt to get better wages and working conditions, to stop wards being closed and patients neglected, they decided to march on the Houses of Parliament. Several were injured at the entrance to Whitehall as Margaret Thatcher drove home her point: She sent the riot police out against them.

That was when I was in Liverpool, and the evening news brought me the haunting image of a nurse pushing ineffectually against a policeman's riot shield. The papers carried that picture the next morning, and somehow, in a still shot, it was even more distressing. Her whole posture spoke despair; she might have been leaning on him for comfort, to be held and consoled.

There used to be strength in the image of the English policeman—strength and decency and security. All that's gone now. The policeman stared out over the nurse's head, impassive, as though unaware that anything at all was on the other side of his shield.

CHIPPED IVORY

OXBRIDGE memories: springtime balls. The May Balls in Cambridge, the Eights Balls in Oxford. Huge green and white striped tents set up in the quads, and the men in full evening dress, the more daring ones with red or white cummerbunds instead of black, and the women in gowns with lots of petticoats and makeup and pearls, the daring ones among them in something simpler, with a big diving V down to the waist in back or even in front, and the champagne flowing and flowers spilling over the tables and big live bands playing frothy music and small live bands trying to imitate the Beatles through until dawn . . .

They are another world, these balls. A world apart from the demise of the welfare state, from economic cutbacks and tearful nurses and bread-and-butter sandwiches and race riots.

Few have been to the balls but everyone knows of them since most of England's best-known writers are Oxbridge products, and like writers everywhere, they obey the injunction to write about what they know. The balls are the very image of privilege and decadence, of the best and the brightest of English minds desperately trying to be witty and drunk at the same time, to be sophisticated and to get laid.

I did the balls in 1962—sweet sixteen, as they say, but with a precocious attraction to the older men of nineteen and twenty already up at Oxbridge. The gritty reality of the northern cities

119

of Liverpool and Manchester was still a year away. I went to two balls that year, one at Oxford, one at Cambridge. I don't remember which colleges, and it really makes little difference, since the two combine in memory into one. Both my dates were studying history. Both would graduate with firsts. Both had excellent prospects.

One was tall, dark, curly haired, and definitely Byronic. He was involved with civil rights in the States and was planning to go to Mississippi that summer and help with voter registration. His friends gathered in his rooms before the ball, and we draped ourselves over the battered leather sofas and downed our Pimms—always Pimms Number One in those days, sweet and potent. The talk was political, committed, heady. Neckties were awry, dress shirts wrinkled above the cummerbunds, hair long and unruly. This group of people would change the world. But I never heard of any of them again.

The other was far more restrained. He talked about nineteenth-century economic history. His friends were just as serious, and dull. They were handsome too—any Oxbridge student was handsome by definition in those days—and their dress was immaculate. We smoked long, thin cigars, no thicker than a cigarette. We were very elegant. He went on to become a diplomat, and it was inconceivable then that ten years later he'd marry an American wife, leave the diplomatic service, and settle in the States.

I remember two dawns: One, walking along chilled to the bone in my flimsy gown, feeling clumsy and awkward and longing for a blanket and bed; the other, punting on the river, laughing, and fishing out the inevitable drunken punters who'd taken a watery fall.

I was too awed by it all for memory to be more precise. This was it: hallowed stones, ivied walls, grassy quads, bicycles and gowns, port and Stilton cheese, the Cam, the Cherwell, the punts, King's College Chapel, the Bodleian Library, lead-paned bow windows, porters, dons, May Balls—the whole giddy elixir of life in the elite, the fast track of English society, the world of Auden's glittering prizes via Frederic Raphael, of Evelyn Waugh's Brideshead follies, of homosexual effetes and Communist elites, of Nobel prizes and great debates and hot buttered crumpets for tea, and above all of talk—the brilliant, sparkling talk of those who knew that simply by virtue of being here, the world was theirs.

Theirs, I sensed, and not mine. For the famous colleges were all male societies. The few women's colleges were grim, staid places, with none of the romantic medieval architecture of the men's ones. They stood apart from the center of things, slightly outside town. They had their own separate tutors and dons, and though just as intellectual, they had none of the excitement. Even then, years before the word feminism came into circulation, I wanted to go to King's, not Girton, to Magdalen and not to Somerville. The women at the Oxbridge balls were mainly nurses and secretarial students at small schools in the towns. Women students were bluestockings. It was a man's world, and I wanted it. With all the absoluteness of my sixteen years, I wanted it all. And if I couldn't have it all, I'd have none of it.

IT is usually assumed in the States that since I'm English and intelligent, I went to Oxbridge. Which I didn't. Though I was intended to.

I was one of the group of students in my school destined for the Oxbridge track—the group the school could proudly point to as proof of its academic excellence. I had no automatic "in." My father hadn't gone to Oxbridge, nor had his father before him, so there was no family tradition to put to work. I'd go in the hard way, on my own merits, passing the entrance examinations for a scholarship. My teachers beamed with anticipation. Nobody asked what I wanted to study once I got there. It was assumed I'd take English.

My rebellion was not well reasoned. It focused on the Latin requirement for entrance in the humanities. I had stopped studying Latin two years before, passing my requisite O-level exam and ritually burning the books afterwards. The reason for that may not have been the language so much as the teacher—a caricature of the English spinster harridan, tall and thin with granny glasses, a high rasping voice, a fondness for the ruler as a means of correction, and a bald spot right on the crown of her frizzy-haired head. She hated children, and we returned the favor. She loved Caesar, and that favor we did not return.

It was a dry, dead love, without a spark to ignite in others. A dead language for a woman dead inside. I practiced the passive resistance known to every schoolchild in every country in the world: I daydreamed. The room in which we studied the Gallic Wars was filled with light, and I spent much of my time in class studying the motes of dust drifting in the air. Other times, I'd run through the list of possible diseases in my father's old medical texts, trying to find the best fit for this woman and ending up with a simple, massive stroke, the medical equivalent of a bolt from the blue.

"You can't go to Oxbridge without Julius Caesar," she crowed, and in the motes of dust I saw myself riding triumphant into that mythical city, crowned with laurel leaves, with all of Caesar's armies riding behind me.

Did I know then what I know now? That an Oxbridge education was a sine qua non if you really wanted to do anything meaningful in England? That *The Times* and the BBC recruited almost solely from Oxbridge, as did the diplomatic service, the civil service, and senior management. That an Oxbridge education meant more than the eminence of an Ivy League one—it was preeminent. That the real agenda of Oxbridge was not education per se, but to instill confidence—a sense of being part of the elite, of everything being open to you, of commanding possibility and ability, and of being indisputably, unarguably, not only English, but the best of the English. It was the first-class ticket into England.

I'm not sure how much a sixteen-year-old knows about his

or her own country. You absorb the values, the mores, without quite being aware of it. I must have known all this, but when I tried to imagine myself at Oxbridge, it was far from another world I was just beginning to discover. My new boyfriend had just been arrested in Red Square for handing out Ban the Bomb leaflets. He came back with a file full of clippings—his pride and joy. We took part in the Aldermaston marches, convinced that if we just shouted loud enough, and walked far enough, we'd rid the world of nuclear weapons. We smoked grass, we made love not war, and we knew that we were the vanguard of a whole new generation.

The peace and quiet of establishment Oxbridge seemed unreal, far removed from all that. The germ of rebellion had taken seed; it was followed through with a teenager's zeal.

I walked into the Latin exam tabula rasa, unsure of what I would do. I took one look at the question paper, studied the ceiling a moment, then took a deep breath, set the paper aside, and wrote a long, well-reasoned essay—or so it seemed to me—on why Latin should not be a necessary requirement for Oxbridge entrance. It was exactly the kind of audacious move that might have gained me entrance—had I written it in Latin. Stubbornly, rebelliously, I wrote it in English.

And with that one essay, I now realize, wrote my ticket out of England. Economy class.

I chose the ground floor over the ivory tower and went up to Manchester, the industrial center of the north, far from the willows and lily pads of the Cam and the Cherwell. When I put out my fingers to touch a white flower, they came away blackened with soot. When I walked through a dense fog, hugging the walls for direction, padded footfalls and hacking coughs sounded unseen around me, and I imagined myself back in Victorian England, in the middle of a Dickens novel.

It was a working-class university at the time, in the middle of one of the worst of Manchester's slums. In fact, it was the main landowner in the area, collecting rents from the brothels along nearby "murder mile." My roommate and I, both well-bred young ladies from the south, stared at it all in wide-eyed fascination, convinced that this was Life. She studied architecture. I had chosen drama.

The appeal was irresistible. The drama department was new; this was the first year. I'd be in right at the beginning, and we'd be building something as we went along, creating our own tradition. In fact, we would *be* the tradition!

At first it was wonderful—a whole group of people walking around in flamboyant dress calling each other "Darling!" all the time. It was all terribly dramatic. Except that there was no drama. Two months later, I fast-talked my way into the psychology department and spent the next three years discovering R. D. Laing, experimenting with LSD, and solving the world's problems through the psychology of conflict and international relations.

It never occurred to me to even think that I could have been studying *Middlemarch* at Oxford, let alone regret it. It was only when I finally read *Middlemarch* many years later, that I realized the full enormity of my escape. Occasionally, I'd see an old school friend who'd made it to Girton or Somerville or one of the other women's Oxbridge colleges. They wore tweeds and pearls, spoke with upper-class accents, and looked slightly appalled at my determinedly bohemian duffel coat and jeans. We lived in different worlds. Theirs led to the core of England. Mine led out.

OVER twenty years later, I walked through the quads of University College, Oxford, in search of Kingman Brewster, the American master of the college until his death in 1988. Keeping carefully off the grass—only dons allowed to set foot on it—I crossed the main quad to staircase seven, then through the inner quad of Radcliffe Court to staircase twelve where I found the secretary's office. A small gate led from there to the ivied Master's Lodgings.

Surrounded by stone, I was well buffered against the reality of the town, let alone of the country or the world. Courts within courts within courts: A don could spend a whole lifetime inside here, entirely in the intellect, with no real contact with the outside world. This was the ivory tower at its highest and purest.

In fact the ivory was old medieval stone. It looked forbiddingly damp, but inside it was comfortably carpeted and centrally heated; the interiors of the colleges were far less shabby than I remembered. Creature comforts had finally made it to Oxford, despite the conversation overheard that morning through the broken panes of a phone box outside the Bodleian Library, a collect call carried on with a strong Midwestern twang:

"You won't believe the facilities here! They're medieval, like really medieval, as old as the college. Like they never heard of the twentieth century, you know? They've got one bathroom for eight people, right? And there's this green mold growing all over the walls, like nobody's cleaned it in four hundred years. And nobody uses electric toothbrushes, can you believe it? And they've never heard of dental floss. And it's so damp the towels never dry, so there's always this weird smell like something real awful's growing in the basement. . . ."

A gaggle of American students walked past the secretary's office as I waited to see Brewster. They were talking—not too loudly, probably, by American standards, but here in this walled retreat of academe their voices rang out. Their scrubbed unselfconscious Americanness seemed completely out of place; their accents weren't clipped, they weren't precise and quiet. Oxford students en groupe talk in a calming murmur; their voices never ring off the stone walls.

I tried to imagine this place populated by Americans and couldn't. That's the supreme thing about Oxford: Above all else, more than Wimbledon or Westminster or Buckingham Palace, this is the essence of old-time England. Which is why Kingman Brewster felt so comfortable here.

Brewster was a New Englander, a former president of Yale,

a former ambassador to Great Britain, and an Anglophile, sold on the old World War Two image of England as the land of selfless public servants, stubborn pluck, bravery, stoicism, and of course, noblesse oblige. Now he'd achieved the fond dream of every English senior civil servant, the pinnacle of a full and devoted career—a house in the rolling Berkshire countryside, and the good-natured ease and elegance of an Oxford mastership.

Perhaps it was to be expected that once I'd settled into one of the well-worn leather armchairs in his study, a Mexican stand-off would develop between us—I, the Briton who felt at home in America, he the American who felt at home in England. Inevitably, perhaps, the conversation halted, stumbled, missed the track, as though we were two transatlantic liners, one going west, the other east, passing each other in mid-ocean.

Instead of exploring the stereotypes of England as the repository of culture and literacy, and America as the center of science, technology, and money, we went veering off in a different direction. He hadn't been in the job too long, but he was beginning to realize why the college was so eager for an American to take the helm at this stage. Oxford needs money.

Margaret Thatcher's cutbacks in education had reached even unto these hallowed walls, and like the best of the old English elite, Brewster detested her. He attacked "the politics of self-interest," and in particular, Thatcher's "vendetta" on the universities, begun when she was minister of education and continued in full force since she'd been prime minister.

Perhaps only a spurned Oxford graduate could have upset the cart so thoroughly, though how spurned a third-term prime minister can feel is another question. Oxford had refused to grant her an honorary doctorate some years before, in her first term as prime minister. In the ensuing controversy, scientists who'd worked with her in the chemistry labs had described her as competent but uninspired. "Conscientious" was the most flattering word they came up with.

In the class system of British higher education, those are

redbrick adjectives, not Oxbridge ones. Thatcher knew an insult when it was thrown in her face, and having conscientiously worked her way up from the middle class to 10 Downing Street, she did not feel bound by any sense of noblesse oblige. Faced with her cutbacks, Oxbridge colleges realized that their ancient endowments would not suffice. They began to set up "development offices" and to start mailings to alumni—to become positively American in their search for funds. Noblesse oblige was nudged aside by lèse-majesté.

This was only the tip of a huge iceberg of change in the whole English educational system since I'd graduated and left the country. Socialist governments in the seventies had reformed the entire system from grade school up, trying to reduce the influence of the elite "public" schools. But the reform, as such reforms often do, had backfired. It sent more students to university, true, by the simple expedient of formally raising the level of technical colleges to that of universities, but still only an appallingly small percentage of English schoolchildren go on to higher education. In the sixties, it was five for every thousand in the population; today, with Thatcher determined to "trim the fat," it is seven for every thousand. That is one of the lowest rates in Europe; in the United States, where entrance requirements are far less stringent than in England, the figure is forty-one per thousand.

Worse, instead of sounding the death knell of the "public" schools, as it was intended to do, the reform strengthened them. It withdrew government funding from the grammar schools—the one alternate route to the top for bright non-elite schoolchildren such as the young Margaret Thatcher—in an effort to force them into becoming comprehensive schools, catering to a broader spectrum of students. The reaction was sadly predictable: The grammar schools turned private. They joined forces with the elite "public" schools in a new union of independent tuition-charging schools. The two-tier system of English secondary education seemed as entrenched as ever.

Announcements of senior public appointments, for instance, still prominently feature the name of the public school attended. In the 1980s, Eton had produced the Lord Chancellor, the chairman of the BBC, the governor of the Bank of England, the editor of *The Times,* the chief of the defense staff, the head of the civil service, and the head of the foreign service. Thatcher may have shocked people by having only one old Etonian in her cabinet and by having several men who had not attended any university at all, let alone Oxbridge, among her senior advisors, but despite her position and power, her challenge remained that of a frustrated outsider. As Anthony Sampson put it in *The Changing Anatomy of Britain:* "After two decades of ambitious innovation, there is still no substitute for antiquity and inherited wealth."

Nevertheless, Oxbridge colleges now take almost half their entrants from government-funded comprehensive schools, while in the sixties the vast majority were still from public schools, with top-heavy representation from the privileged bastions of Eton, Winchester, and company. Moreover, the Oxbridge men's colleges began to admit women in the seventies, even though the percentages are still heavily male weighted. Even so, this means that over half of Oxbridge students still come from only six percent of the nation's schools—the tuition-charging ones. And despite the eight new universities set up along American lines in the late sixties and early seventies to challenge Oxbridge supremacy, Oxbridge still rules the roost.

"At Oxbridge you're educated to a sense of 'can do,' " said a friend who graduated from Oxford in the sixties, "whereas everywhere else, you are instilled with the feeling of 'can't do.' Oxbridge opens up the world for you; without it, the world remains a closed system. It gives you the sense of 'we're okay, and everyone else is not okay.' The sheer waste of brainpower and potential is just incredible."

As her language shows, she's spent time in the States. "What I like about the States is the sense that 'we're all okay, we're all entitled.' It doesn't work entirely, of course, but compared to the English system, it's a huge contrast."

Thatcher's challenge is very much an American one; her ideal is a meritocracy to replace the aristocracy. Whether she'll succeed may depend on the staying power of her economic revolution. The more successful her economic policies, the better her chances of making her criticisms of Oxbridge stick. They are too oriented to the humanities, she charges. Too disdainful of business and industry. Too ivory tower, in fact. They may turn out the top minds of England, but those minds have no idea how to bend themselves around creative financing or innovative business ideas.

The proof, as they say in the north of England, is in the pudding. England's top industrialists are not and never have been Oxbridge men. Many have never been to university at all. Some, like Sir James Goldsmith, or Robert Maxwell, were not even born in England. Upstart foreigners, they didn't feel inhibited by the English class system of can do and can't do. In fact, the one detail of Goldsmith's life most fascinating to Britons is that he dropped out of Eton, which on the scale of things English is tantamount to throwing your silver spoon to the birds.

As England struggled up out of the financial recession of the seventies, new money began to challenge entrenched class, threatening not only Oxbridge but that other bastion of upper-class self-interest, the City of London, where the Big Bang means that you don't have to be upper class to make money anymore.

I was vaguely aware that bringing up a subject such as the Big Bang in the master's study of University College, Oxford was somewhat inappropriate, rather like bringing a shovel of dirt into a Belgravia drawing room. But Kingman Brewster, after all, was a cosmopolitan man, and no American ambassador to the Court of St. James, let alone a lawyer by training and profession, could afford to ignore the power of the financial markets. So I wasn't prepared for his reaction.

In his comfortable study, surrounded by leather-bound tomes and the ancient solidity of stone, Kingman Brewster shook his head at the idea of greed run rampant in the City. Speaking in his clipped New England accent—the most acceptable of American accents to the English, since the closest to the English one—and with a frown as disapproving as that of the most dowager of English duchesses, he said; "It's not British, you know. It's just not British."

I could only nod in response. After all, that was the whole point. That's what made the Big Bang so exciting.

I took the back way from University College through to St. John's, walking between high stone walls where it was quiet and peaceful. I was on my way to lunch with a friend who's a don there. More quads, monastic covered walks, Gothic windows. If you want to, you can spend your whole life as a don staying inside your college as though it was a monastery. You can retreat from the world, with all your needs—food, shelter, livelihood—taken care of.

In the wood-paneled commons of St. John's—the commons being most uncommon, since it is the dons' dining room—the huge U-shaped oak refectory table could seat fifty easily in leather and wood dining chairs nicely battered from generations of intellectual backsides. The whole room had that air of shabby elegance and genteel decay that is the ultimate in upper-class Englishness—the mark of real privilege. Dress as well as manner seemed relaxed, though under the table the hands betrayed the tension. Some were prim and neatly folded, others almost clenched into fists.

The food was better than tradition once dictated. The vegetables were still boiled to pale wateriness but the Stilton was superb. But then, of course, the Stilton has always been superb.

Inevitably, we compared transatlantic notes. My friend had

spent some time in the States and had great difficulty readjusting to Oxford on his return.

"Everything was so open and energetic there," he said. "If you had a good idea, and the energy to promote it, you'd get the funding and go ahead. It took me time to get used to the Oxford system again. You know, 'We just don't do things that way here.' Oxford hadn't changed, and it wasn't going to. I came back into a closed, set system."

He looked around at the Gothic windows, the waiters with their silver serving dishes, the old oil paintings on the walls, and smiled. "But you get used to it again," he said. "It may not be so stimulating, but it's very comfortable." Only in his mid-thirties, he seemed to have made a compromise, forfeiting intellectual ambition for comfort. I found it strangely unsettling.

We talked about the brain drain: the fact that many of England's best brains, from every university including Oxford and Cambridge, have crossed the Atlantic in search of better pay, better positions, more flexibility, more stimulation. They found them, and stayed. He blamed Margaret Thatcher, but admitted that the brain drain had begun long before she came to power. There were too many good minds impatient with the idea that "we don't do things that way here," eager for a more flexible intellectual environment that would encourage and reward initiative. The drain was especially bad in the sciences: When a top scientist could earn three times the salary and work with the latest equipment in the States, what could keep him in England?

The question was dramatically reiterated as we said goodbye in front of the college gate. A bicycle was making for us along the pavement, veering madly from side to side, scattering pedestrians as the rider raced to tell my friend his news. He was a final-year student, the best in his class, and he was quite literally shaking with excitement—so excited, in fact, that every single atom of him seemed to be alive with it. His hair was all awry, his face flushed, his hands shaking, his eyes shining, and even before he'd stopped his bike, practically knocking us over in the process, his good news was bubbling out of him.

I recognized the accent immediately. Three years at Oxford had made only the slightest dent in the warm Liverpool burr. This was no public schoolboy, but a working-class northern lad who'd made his way to Oxford on merit alone through the comprehensive system, who'd defied the class system and the restrictions of privilege and money and worked his way to this moment he'd dreamed of for years.

The news poured out of him in one long, steady stream of words, almost without a pause for breath.

"I got it!" he said. "I got the grant! There's only five of them in the world in computer simulations of the brain, and I got one! God, do you know what this means? I'll be able to do the doctorate the way I always wanted to, working with the supercomputers! I'll be able to do that whole program we talked about. I'll have the access, and the funding, and I can design the whole program myself. I'll have the freedom to do it, really do it! And I'll be able to travel and work with the very best people in the field. I can hardly believe it, it's what I always dreamed about. It's all come true! And they say that once I've done that, I can name my price. I can do anything I want, they say, any way I want!"

His eyes gleamed, his face flushed even more, and he became still more breathless as he reached the peak of his announcement, the pinnacle of his aspirations. "I can go anywhere," he concluded triumphantly. "I can go to America!"

CLASS WARFARE

AS the time for my Green Card interview grew closer, I became increasingly conscious of my odd status in England—a visitor in my own country, returned to it in order to leave for good. Inevitably, I seemed to see it from both inside and outside at the same time, as though I were of it and yet not of it. And it occurred to me that this was the situation of the spy: I was moving through the country as though it were mine, yet my loyalties were elsewhere, across the Atlantic.

Considering the English talent for masking and subterfuge, this was not as uncomfortable a position as it might seem. England is kind to spies. In fact, it loves them. There's nothing like a really good spy story to get the juices flowing and add some color to a drab English winter. Perhaps that's why the best spy novelists are invariably English; you could say it comes with the territory.

But really devoted enthusiasts of the clandestine follow the real thing. After all, no fiction can ever come up with anything quite as good as the Philby-Burgess-Maclean case, when it took twenty years for British intelligence to wake bleary-eyed to the fact that some of its most senior personnel were Soviet double agents.

They were the cream of England—upper-class and Cambridge educated. Recruited, in fact, while they were students at Cambridge in the early thirties. While Oxbridge students today look to America for their future, in the thirties the fashion was to look to the Soviet Union. And the Soviets took brilliant advantage of that.

Oxford and Cambridge were more elitist then than now. The middle class was expected to go elsewhere. Working class need not apply. Their graduates had an automatic "in" with the British foreign and secret services. They were "our kind of people" to those who ran the small and clubby intelligence services, meaning upper-class, well connected, and imbued with a sense of their own social, moral, and intellectual superiority. They belonged to the right clubs, talked with the right accents, lived in the right places.

It seemed perfectly natural to those in charge of intelligence to bring in those who were "their kind." So natural, in fact, that they did no security checks. So natural, indeed, that even though they knew some of their new recruits had been openly Communist at Cambridge, they paid no attention. "Youthful enthusiasm," they said to each other in their London clubs. "Perfectly understandable." "He'll settle down." "Good man—knew his father at King's, you know."

Faced with such upper-class complacency, the Soviets could hardly resist. Beyond the practical matter of gaining information at the highest levels, there must have been a particular satisfaction in penetrating the class system so effectively and so deliciously—using the upper class against itself.

By the late forties, the Soviet penetration was in high gear. Donald Maclean, probably the most committed ideological Communist of the three, was in the British Embassy in Washington, quietly and systematically transferring top-level American nuclear information to the Soviets.

The flamboyant Guy Burgess was an intelligence gadfly, flitting around between the various branches of the system, doing odd jobs. He was so obviously a security risk that nobody thought he could be one. After all, like the others he was a Cambridge graduate, part of the elite Apostles group there. Impossible that he not be trustworthy, no matter how embarrassing his drunken bouts, his sexual encounters with young boys, his brushes with the police.

Of the three, Philby was clearly the most dangerous. The son of Harry St. John Philby, whose fame as a desert explorer and Arabist was bested only by that of his friend T. E. Lawrence, he was named after the hero of Rudyard Kipling's novel *Kim*—a young boy who serves his country as a spy. On his father's part, that was evidently tempting fate. In fact, Philby senior probably relished the irony for he too was a man of double roles, and in 1930 he resigned from the British foreign service, became a Muslim, and took the name of Haj Abdullah.

Orphaned as an Englishman, as it were, the younger Philby was recruited by Soviet intelligence soon after, and then by British intelligence too. By the end of World War Two he had set up the MI-6 section that spied on the Soviet Union and was head of its entire counterespionage operation. Which meant that the Soviets were running British counterespionage against themselves.

Philby was awarded the Order of the British Empire for his superb work and was generally considered next in line to become the chief of MI-6. By the time he sent Burgess and Maclean running for Moscow, he was not only head of the British liaison with American intelligence, he was also a full colonel in the KGB.

In short, Kim Philby was the most successful mole ever—or at least the most successful mole ever uncovered. John Le Carré remained deeply in his debt throughout his "Smiley" novels, as did that other grand master of fictional subterfuge, Graham Greene, who had once worked under Philby and even visited him in Moscow after his defection. Like a spy, a novelist never lets go of a good source.

All three spies defected to Moscow before they could be interrogated—Burgess and Maclean in 1951, and Philby in 1963—placing the British intelligence partnership with the Americans in open jeopardy. The official British reaction was to close ranks, to keep things quiet, to maintain the highest secrecy about the most astounding intelligence penetration in modern history. As a result of which there has been a continuous stream of revelations about "the Cambridge spies" ever since.

Like all of England, I've followed these revelations with fascination, as though if we could understand what made these men betray their country, we'd understand something about the country itself and about ourselves in it. The spies have died meanwhile—Philby was the last to die, in 1988—but death has had no effect on the case's obsessive hold on the English imagination. For over three decades, investigative reporters have kept it a hotselling item, amassing a huge archive of articles and books, each one with that much more titillating detail about the astonishing complacency of the British intelligence community or the flagrant homosexuality of some of the major characters.

Not the least of these details, until 1979, was the persistent rumor of a fourth man who had alerted Philby and enabled him to defect in time, and who had helped recruit the others.

When he was uncovered, the fourth man turned out to be the most revealing of all. What he revealed was England and the class system at its most unpleasant.

Sir Anthony Frederick Blunt, surveyor of the Queen's pictures and director of London's prestigious Courtauld Institute of Art, was a brilliant art historian. He had also been a "talent spotter" for Soviet intelligence when he was a don at Cambridge University in the thirties. He worked for British intelligence from 1940 to 1945, and in that time passed information regularly to the Soviets. But all this was only rumor until 1979, when imminent press disclosure forced Margaret Thatcher to tell Parliament that Blunt had confessed—not recently, but fifteen years earlier, in 1964. And had been promised immunity from prosecution for his confession.

The scandal was delicious. There were questions and more questions: Should he have been promised immunity? How much did the Queen know? How could such a traitor be handled with kid gloves?

Were it not for the fact that journalists were hot on his heels, Blunt would have died as respected and publicly honored an Englishman as ever could be. Instead he died discredited, stripped of his knighthood, and under constant siege from the press.

Even his name was deceptive. There was nothing common about Anthony Blunt. He was as establishment as any Englishman can possibly be. He had "all the advantages of life," as the English say—everything going for him. A Cambridge education, membership in the elite Apostles club, and entry into the highest levels of society, from the Foreign Office to Buckingham Palace.

He was also, as his close friend Louis MacNeice put it, a man with "a flair for bigotry." A man who didn't give a fig, let alone anything else, for the working class or the huddled masses of Communist ideology. A man who, his defenders argued, began to spy for the Soviets in the thirties in order to counter British appeasement of the Nazis, but whose act of conscience, if so, survived the Hitler-Stalin pact intact.

Other defenders said he spied because of his homosexuality, as though all homosexuals were potential spies, or as though upper-class England was not pervasively homosexual and infinitely kinder to homosexuals than the Soviet Union. He was seduced by Guy Burgess, they said, entranced by the other man's flagrant mooning of all the values held dear by the establishment—discretion, repression, inhibition. But in fact it's unlikely that Burgess and he ever had a physical relationship. Like Burgess, this dry devotee of the esthetic was obsessed with rough trade—quick, anonymous sex with working-class lads in underground public toilets.

Above all—far above all—Anthony Blunt was an arrogant snob. A man who despised anything beneath him, as most of England was. A man for whom the idea of loyalty must have been "so bourgeois, my dear"—an idea of the common folk, a little myth to glue them together in a gelatinous undifferentiated mass, like lumpy lukewarm porridge served in a railway station cafeteria. Yet a man in thrall to the very idea of the royal family, whose retainer he became as the Queen's art advisor, thus earning his knighthood.

Anthony Blunt could not have survived in any other country, but he could probably not have been created in any other, either. He could only have been English, and English at its worst.

Even those who spoke in his defense painted a ghastly cameo portrait. Here is art critic Brian Sewell in a letter to *The Sunday Times* in 1981—two years after Blunt had been publicly exposed and his knighthood withdrawn—explaining that Blunt had deliberately misled the newspaper on a certain detail in order to draw attention away from a friend.

"Anthony is convinced that the story will be made to seem discreditable," wrote Sewell. "It is characteristic of him that he would use that word, and care deeply about it, in the matter of a personal relationship, while not caring at all for what others might conceive as discreditable in a larger sense. Unlike ordinary mortals whose levels of response are either single or interwoven, Anthony has an ice-cold strain to his nature that is separate from his functions as an art historian and an affectionate and lively human being."

It was a breathtaking sketch of Anthony Blunt, *übermensch.*

"As it turned out, none of us knew him," said another friend after it was all over—Blunt died of a heart attack in 1983 to the immense relief of the security services and the government. But none of them *could* know him. There was no him to know. Ironically, it took an émigré Russian, Nobel-prizewinning writer Joseph Brodsky, to point this out.

Blunt couldn't have cared less about Marxism, said Brodsky. It had all been done for the exhilaration of it. For the clandestine excitement. As a favor to friends. A proclivity for manipulating people. An indulgence. It was impossible to find the real Blunt: "He was a good example of what is known as negative reality.

Nothing, not his books, his lecture notes, or anecdotes from family, friends, lovers or enemies, could ever give him substance." Not even to himself.

Perhaps only a superb novelist could fathom Anthony Blunt. Fiction frees you from the realm of anecdote, taking you into the soul of a character. What makes someone turn on their own country? Is there something in England itself that engenders it? Does the subterfuge and masking of everyday communication and existence create the ideal personality for a spy?

For someone who turned her back on England over twenty years ago—someone wandering now through the country, feeling as though she were spying on herself—such questions are irresistible.

The novelist who comes closest to an answer is John Le Carré, whose work far surpasses the "thriller" genre, and whose understanding of the psyche of the spy has never been as acute or as detailed as in his 1986 novel, *A Perfect Spy*. By no coincidence, it was also the first le Carré novel to carry a full-face photograph of the author, who until then had refused to pose except in shadowy profile. This was a novel, he knew, of revelation.

Le Carré's perfect spy is Magnus Pym, so perfect that the word *spy* is hidden in his name as in a cryptic crossword clue. Pym is the quintessence of upper-class Englishness, though his upper-classness is revealed as a con, dreamed up and created by his con-man father.

The metaphor could not be better. Spying, after all, is a sophisticated con. Instead of stealing money, the spy steals secrets. If he's a master of the art, he even uses the same techniques—flattery, love, trust, promises. And like a double agent, the analogy works on a dual level: Since Pym's utter Englishness is itself a con, the novel becomes a portrait of the Englishman as con man.

To understand the spy, you must crack the code that made him. Le Carré never bought into the theory that the Cambridge spies turned double agents because of their concern about English appeasement of Hitler. He looked inward, not outward. And found his point of contrast in America, where Pym is posted for a time to the British Embassy.

America challenges the Englishman. "He set out to disbelieve everything he saw. He found no holding point, no stern judgement to revolt against. These vulgar, pleasure-seeking people, so frank and clamorous, were too uninhibited for his shielded and convoluted life. They loved their prosperity too obviously, were too flexible and mobile, too little the slaves of place, origin and class. They had no sense of that hush which all Pym's life had been the background music of his inhibition."

A key word to the code here—inhibition. And another one—hush. All Britons have disembodied childhood memories of people hushing them. "Shhh." "Don't be flamboyant." "Don't be enthusiastic." "Don't show."

Poor Pym, so English in America: "He wanted his dreadful schools back. He wanted everything but the marvelous horizons that led to lives he had not lived. He wanted to spy upon hope itself, look through keyholes at the sunrise and deny the possibilities he had missed." And as he does so, he feels the inhibition temporarily melting. In a Disneyland projection room, watching the American dream unfold on the screen, he dissolves into a cynical sentimentality—an oxymoron, true, but not for an Englishman.

"Pym never felt more free in his life. . . . Everything he still contrived to love in himself was here to love in the people around him. A willingness to open themselves to strangers. A guile that was only there to protect their innocence. A fantasy that fired but never owned them. A capacity to be swayed by everything, while still remaining sovereign."

Another key word here—love. Pym didn't spy for ideology. Nor for money. Nor for any of the other usual reasons associated with treason. Not because he hated his country, nor because he loved the Communist bloc. He spied for love—not for sexual love, but in the final analysis for self-love. His own self was so deeply repressed, pushed down so far inside him, that the only self he knew lay in the various roles he played for others. He could see himself only as reflected in the admiration of others, and his desperate need to be loved by all made him loyal to none.

In this, Le Carré is a romantic. Pym is a bewildered, sympathetic character, the calculating coldness of his actions made human by his need for love. He doesn't bleed, but somewhere deep inside him something leaks, slowly, inexorably, like blood. Those who are easy to betray are no problem—he is fond of them, but does not really love them. His only true love is the one man who knows his capacity for betrayal—his Czech controller. Find Pym out and he is yours for life. Except that to do that, you have to outplay him at his own game. You have to be a better con man than he.

Anthony Blunt, by comparison, seems utterly cold-blooded. But though the one is sympathetic and the other totally unsympathetic, the fictional and nonfictional characters have a lot in common. There is that sheer intellectual challenge of walking the tightrope—playing off one role against the other, raising the ante of inevitable discovery. Blunt did in politics what he did in the public toilets: He courted danger and experienced the exhilaration of evasion. But above all, he acted out a basic duality—the essence of a successful double agent's life—in an almost schizoid split in which the spy takes revenge on the Englishman, while the Englishman never loses his grip.

It would be kind to think that in his own way Blunt was only doing what the lower-class football hooligans do: rebelling against the mask, and trying, in destructive and self-destructive ways, to break it. It could be seen, perhaps, like many failed suicides are seen—as a cry for help, a recognition of restriction, and a desperate attempt to break out of it. Or it could be seen more cold-bloodedly as an act of derision and contempt—and if so, then also an act of self-derision and self-contempt.

Blunt was a man utterly of his class, working for a system devoted to the destruction of that class. Everything he cherished and prized—the rarefied world of art appreciation, the elite circles of royalty, the advantages and connections of upper-class privilege—was anathema in Soviet society. By working for the Soviets he worked against himself and against all he stood for. Against his own snobbery, his own refinement, his own sense of superiority.

In recruiting him, the Soviets evidently understood the class system and its casualties better than the English did. What they perceived—and what the English couldn't—was that class contorts and distorts individuals throughout the social spectrum, at the top as much as at the bottom. From their point of view, Anthony Blunt was probably just another victim of class.

TITLED DREAMS

"NOW then," declared the dance teacher in her fruity voice, "today we're going to learn how to be presented to the Queen."

She dismissed the logistic details of becoming a debutante and being presented at Court—the requirements of birth, connections, and so on—with a theatrically gracious wave of her right hand. Small and swaybacked, Miss Biddlecombe's dreams of a great ballet career had long been sublimated into fantasies of the success of her protégées.

We looked at each other in bored confusion. We were a bunch of unruly, round-shouldered ten-year-olds. We knew perfectly well that the likelihood of any of us ever becoming a debutante was very close to zero.

"We start," she said, "with The Curtsy."

It went like this:

You enter from stage right, taking two long steps. . . .

"Slowly, very slowly," said Miss Biddlecombe. "And gracefully. Stretch out your arms, now. Yes, that's it. Remember your gown . . ."

You are very careful to allow room for the huge gown you are wearing, taffeta and silk and sequins having miraculously sprouted over your school uniform. All graciousness, you spread your arms out over it, then take the next step with your right foot crossed in front of your left.

"That's it, right across left. No, in front of the left, not behind it. In front, I said. In front."

You cross your right in front of the left, then, leaving you awkwardly cross-legged in mid-stride.

"Keep your balance, now . . . No! Get up, girl! Really! Stop giggling and do it again!"

Next comes a regular step followed by another cross-legged one, this time with the right foot behind the left. Left behind right, right behind left. Your tongue works out of your mouth in concentration as you try to get it right.

"Look up, girls. Up! Not at the floor! Look at me, I'm the Queen, and you must never take your eyes off me. Never. That's terribly rude."

By this time you are inevitably stuck in one cross-legged posture or another.

"Oh, why can't you all do it like Joan does . . ."

Thus sealing Joan's fate after class. Then you come to the really hard part: the long slow wobble downwards, right leg locked behind left.

"Heads *up,* I said. Up!"

Your hands are supposed to be gracefully outstretched on either side, but instead they're flapping at the end of crazily windmilling arms as you struggle for balance in the descent down to the floor, and though you're supposed to hold the curtsy there, in deep obeisance, you can't. As though coming up for air after a dive into a pool, your arms propel you upward again. Miss Biddlecombe tilts at you, straightens your hands, raises your head, rearranges your legs, and suddenly you lose all balance and topple over in another fit of giggles as she tut-tuts:

"I just don't know what young ladies have come to nowadays."

And order having been restored, you still face the task of moving offstage without tripping over your voluminous gown. Another series of cross-legged strides, left behind right, right behind left, and finally:

"Exit left. Yes! That's it! Perfect!"

The Curtsy: Given a good drink and a certain amount of raucous encouragement, I can still do it, complete with all my adolescent wobbles, though the whole absurd scenario no longer takes place. They stopped presenting debutantes at Court some time in the sixties, another sign that things would never be quite the same again. And the Miss Biddlecombes of England went the way of all flesh, decaying, I imagine, into heaps of lavender-scented dust.

What was she thinking of? What fantasy was she indulging? What little luxury of escape, as the tinny out-of-tune piano echoed off the tired wood paneling and the floor vibrated with the thumps of clod-footed children trampling over each other's feet? Her job was to teach us the waltz and the fox-trot and whatever social graces came with them, but in her lonely bed at night she surely dreamed of dancing the lead at Covent Garden —Giselle, the dying swan, the wood nymph. She dreamed of the accolades as the audience stood in ovation, calling her back again and again. Of a stage strewn with roses. And the pinnacle of it all: Her Majesty—herself, mind you, in the flesh—coming back-stage, raising her up from the deep curtsy to the floor with her own hand, and in a slow, sonorous pronouncement, declaring her Dame Edith Biddlecombe.

Miss Biddlecombe's dreams: the dreams of England in the fifties. Sweeping staircases were made for her dreams. Fred Astaire was made for her dreams. The royal family were made for her dreams . . .

THEY were part of our lives yet set totally apart from us. The Queen's coronation in 1952 was a holiday, a huge event in my childhood, marked by the purchase of our first television set so that we could watch the ceremonies and listen to Richard Dimbleby's commentary.

It had to be Dimbleby. Dimbleby *was* the BBC. Imagine

Walter Cronkite if CBS were the only network in the States—the one voice that could reach into every household in the nation—and you have an idea of how central Dimbleby was. The coronation could not have been held without him, or so it seemed. And when Charles married Di, there were many who muttered that it just wasn't the same without that famous voice on the commentary. It wasn't quite right, as though the master of ceremonies had slipped up and forgotten to raise Dimbleby from the dead for the event.

He managed to give everything the appropriate sense of ceremony. Without that, royalty could easily pall. Like the time the Queen Mother came to visit Reading.

I have no idea why she did, and at age seven it didn't matter. What mattered was that it was a holiday. We were taken out of school and lined up along the streets, given little paper Union Jacks on wooden sticks to hold, and told to wave them as the Queen Mother drove by in her carriage. Except that when she did drive by, an hour later, few of us remembered to wave. We stood there, open-mouthed, wondering why this little old woman in an open carriage seemed so utterly familiar. One look, and we knew her. We knew she smelled of lavender water. We knew the dryness of her skin, the lace trim on her handkerchief, the little violet comfit candies in a tiny enameled box at the bottom of her handbag. We knew her for the archetype of the English grandmother.

There was no Dimbleby to heighten it for us, to give us the sense of occasion. We needed his voice: "And what a dream the Queen Mother does look in her powder blue hat trimmed with baby ostrich feathers." We needed to hear that mix of admiration and condescension, of familiarity and slack-jawed gaping, which is how the English generally relate to the royal family or, as they are more often called, "the royals."

I wouldn't marry Prince Charles if he asked me," I was saying. "Shaking hands for a living? It's a terrible job."

146

A gasp went round the New York broadcast studio. I was supposed to be talking about something else altogether, but the previous topic on this particular talk show—*the* topic on every talk show in the city that week, in fact—had been the engagement of Charles and Di, and everyone had been so deadeningly sober and serious about it that it seemed to me some levity was sorely needed.

"Besides," I added, "it's a bad bloodline. Too much inbreeding, you know. Look at those huge ears! That receding chin! Imagine the children!"

"You're not serious," said the interviewer. He looked truly shocked. I had to remind myself that I was talking about the heir apparent of England, not America.

"You know, not everybody in England is crazy about the royals," I went on. "In fact there's a sizeable sector of opinion which thinks they should be abolished."

"Abolished!" From his expression you'd have thought there'd never been an American Revolution.

America is entranced with British royalty. Movie stars are as close as America gets to royalty, and though the Hollywood myth endures, it still cannot requite the longing for something older—the hankering for palaces and castles, fortresses and moats, kings and queens, wizards and magicians, dungeons and dragons. It's a longing for fairy-tale fantasy, for an old world of benign dictatorships where kings and queens ruled over loyal subjects and the wicked wizard would perish in the end. It's a yearning, in fact, for everything Europe struggled to emancipate itself from.

The American romance with royalty began, perhaps, with the seduction of the once and future king by "that American adventuress," as she was known in England, Mrs. Wallis Simpson. Suddenly, royalty became attainable. Even if it meant abdication, at least there was a dukedom in the offing. Americans were seduced as thoroughly as Edward VIII. Confusing titular nobility with the real thing, they ignored the unpleasant reality of the Duke and Duchess of Windsor, whose evident right-wing prejudices and sympathies for Hitler were smothered by reams of romantic fantasy.

The fantasy wore far better in the States than in England. When Sotheby's decided to sell the Duchess's jewelry in 1988, they made a judicious evaluation of the economic power of the myth and decided to hold the auction in New York instead of London.

The English fact of things is that like everything else the royals are not what they used to be. As the twentieth century reaches its end, noblesse oblige has become more obviously oblige and far less noblesse. It was probably always that way, but so long as the royals were safe from the eye of the television camera, they could get away with it.

Their mistake was to allow the cameras in. To permit the close-up.

It began in the early seventies when some bright young thing on the palace staff decided that the Queen's Christmas Day speech to the nation needed to be a bit livelier. At first blush, this might seem an interesting proposition. The trouble with it was that it missed the whole point of the tradition.

The speech is an intrinsic part of Christmas Day, coming right after lunch, just as everyone sits back replete with turkey and Christmas pudding and brandy butter, bodies and minds so sated with heavy cloying food that nobody has the slightest critical capacity left. There is never anything of import in the speech, of course. The Queen is not allowed to say anything of importance. But the ritual phrases—the opening "my husband and I" is the most famous—go down well after the Christmas pud. Tradition, after all, is tradition.

And to mess with tradition is folly.

Nevertheless, the decision was made: A short documentary to go with the speech, one of those just-another-family kind of documentaries intended to humanize the royals.

It worked all too well. The whole of England was treated to the mundane inanities of family life in the palace. Suddenly—

horror!—ordinary people could identify with people who were supposed to be extraordinary.

Worse still, having once committed themselves to camera without ceremony, the royal family had no excuse to keep other cameras away. The press leaped. And the once-tender fantasies of the Miss Biddlecombes of England now became an ongoing soap opera for the whole world. The most expensive soap opera ever, moreover, and with what a cast!

First, of course, the matriarch: the Queen. She's the richest woman in the world, valued, they say, at about five billion pounds sterling. That in itself should suffice to make her glamorous, yet she stunningly, stubbornly, resists. Her self-assigned role is the incarnation of traditional values and respectability. She's necessary to the story line, and of course to the bloodline, but her only real interest is who will succeed her, and when. Other than that, the only drama written into her script in recent years was when a rather disturbed young man broke into her bedroom at Buckingham Palace. The public responded more with puzzlement than shock. Why on earth would anyone *want* to break into the Queen's bedroom?

Then there's the tragic sister, Princess Margaret. A much meatier role here, as she sacrificed her love life for her country, denying herself fulfillment in marriage to a dashing—and divorced—young fighter pilot, and then, oh lord, marrying a photographer instead, albeit one with a double-barreled name and without a divorce behind him. This dangerous dip into the world of the commoner was covered up quickly by a peerage; Antony Armstrong-Jones became Lord Snowdon and the marriage was everyone's ideal romance until, as ideal romances do, it ended. Not the marriage, mind you, only the romance. This is the beauty of a royal soap opera—nobody can get divorced. So we have a built-in cast of glamorous figures trapped in unhappy marriages, torn between passion and duty, between smiling public graciousness and heart-rending private agony. And all, oh delight, in the era of zoom lenses and paparazzi.

Snap! Pictures of Meg on Caribbean islands with various well-built young gentlemen of stylish names but uncertain means. Snap! Pictures of Meg reeling, drunken. Snap! Pictures of Meg's black-ringed eyes. Silence. No pictures of Meg as the family hides her away and rumors abound until they manage to pull her back into line. Everyone waits eagerly for her to fall again.

Meanwhile, her niece, Princess Anne, nurses her resentment. Deprived by male siblings of any but the most remote aspirations to the throne—deprived, in fact, even by her own male offspring who rank higher in the line of succession than she herself—Anne takes over the Margaret role, but with considerably less aplomb. The country watches aghast as she falls off her horse in a point-to-point race, arms and legs flailing. It clucks at the sulky, resentful face, which only seems to look right when swathed in a Liberty silk scarf printed with horses and spurs. It listens in horror as she bumbles into the AIDS tragedy, ignorance flying at full mast, to declare the disease "a self-inflicted home goal for the human race." If she continues in this way, she has the potential of becoming the wicked witch of the family.

The male lead is of course the heir apparent, Charles, the dashing Prince of Wales. Never mind his looks or his personality, the Prince of Wales is always dashing by definition.

Snap! Pictures of Charles dancing with bare-breasted beauties in Australia, in Polynesia, anywhere far enough away for the nipples to be invisible. Snap! Pictures of Charles getting on and off navy boats. Snap! Pictures of Charles all togged up for the great outdoors.

In fact he was considered a bit of a klutz by one and all, and somewhat on the flaky side with his talk of health foods and vague pantheistic mysticism. Things looked worrisome for a while until the search for a virgin future queen brought him his little nursery maid. Not so little, since she's an inch or two taller than he, but otherwise ideal. She is made for the myth.

The whole wonderful fantasy of a common girl made into a queen overnight sprouted wings as large as the long dragonfly wings on her wedding dress. Not quite common—an earl or two in the family and all that—but she seemed such a nice girl, a girl you could relate to, shy and sweet and so very pretty. Suddenly, England was full of look-alikes as shop girls and nursery maids adopted Di hairstyles.

But the most perfect touch was Di's godmother: Barbara Cartland, no less—the berouged, beribboned, belaced queen of the romance novel, the unchallenged empress of shop girls' dreams ruling with powdered hanky over her rhinestone realm. Snap, snap, snap! Pictures of Barbara Cartland in her boudoir. She writes in bed, propped up on countless silk pillows with lacy borders, and you can almost smell the expensive French perfumes that seem so much like lavender and rosewater. From her boudoir she reigns over her goddaughter's transformation, like a camp fairy godmother over Cinderella.

But wait! There are evil forces at work, challenging Cartland's magic, and we witness the wonderful, delicious, irresistible transformation from naïf to bitch as Di finds out that marriage is not the answer to her dreams. She grows dangerously thin— anorexia? bulimia? some tragic disease?—then becomes pregnant and faints. Faints, by George, just like in Victorian days! All England watches with bated breath as Charles and Di fight it out beneath masks of fixed smiles and polite gestures.

Snap! They're going to separate! Snap! They've never been happier. Snap! They're giving each other dirty looks. Snap! They're going on a second honeymoon. Poor dear, it's the pressure of the royal life, you know—she wasn't brought up to it, not trained for it. She'll adapt. She'll grow into the role.

Charles complains—to the press—of being a frog trapped in a prince's body. He wants to be a man of the people, he wants to do good, he wants to make a difference. Occasionally he opens his mouth about "an issue"—modern architecture is one of his favorites. The British architectural establishment gets quite huffy about this. Princes, they make it clear, should learn to keep their place. Like children they should be seen and not heard.

Of course Charles could always just pack it in, resign, abdicate, renounce his title, and wearing a tailor-made hair shirt, walk the Scottish Highlands alone for the rest of his life. Good lord, he could even work! But this doesn't seem to occur to him. Instead, he goes skiing in Switzerland and tramping in Scotland, wondering if he'll ever be king and if he'll be able to complain about that too. After all, being king is another of those things that ain't what it used to be.

Meanwhile, back in the palace, his younger brother Andrew begins to look almost dashing, consorting with exotic dancers with names like Koo. Princess Koo? It just wouldn't do. Enter, stage left, salvation in the irrepressible, fun loving, bouncy, exuberant form of Fergie, the Lady Sarah Ferguson. Another royal wedding and it looks like a jolly good time for all. The "young royals" take to dressing up and putting on amateur-hour productions for charity—all in a good cause even if it is, ahem, somewhat sophomoric. Like the time Andrew is off doing his bit for the country, manfully wielding the controls of naval fighter planes, and Fergie and Di have a field day at Ascot. Bored by the races, OD'd on champagne, they pass the time by poking passersby in the backside with their shooting sticks.

"High jinks!" says the popular press. "What fun!" The tonier newspapers snobbishly disagree, noting a certain lack of, well, class, in the young royals. The popular press rightly decries such snobbery, since it should be perfectly obvious that the royal family are not particularly classy. They are, you see, beyond class. Just like J.R. Just like Alexis.

Which is why the royals have become so popular in the United States. Judith Krantz can only weep. The home of the soap opera could hardly resist these Old World fairy tales for New World dreamers: Di's story—what happens to Cinderella after she gets her prince; Charles's story—the caring, man-of-the-people frog trapped in a prince's body, bound in irrevocable marriage to a woman who doesn't understand him; Fergie's story—the

152

breath of fresh air, daring and unconventional, who just loves a good time . . .

These are not people to be curtsied to. They are too familiar, too real. It's too easy to imagine them appearing on "Donahue," answering questions about their favorite movies or jokingly parrying queries about family squabbles. Popularization has democratized them. It's destroyed the essential element of any self-respecting royalty, the unquestioning faith in the superiority of royal blood. Just as any American can identify with the inner life of a movie star, they can now identify with the inner life of a prince.

AMERICA yearns for royalty. Not the old-fashioned, distant kind, but the kind it can relate to. The kind that comes over well on television. The modern British kind.

There is an American version of it in the presidency—not the homey simplicity of the Carter White House, but the delighted acclaim accorded the Reagan one, with Ronnie's affable showmanship and Nancy's glitzy evening dresses. The only trouble was that Americans took it seriously.

The United States proclaims its democracy loudly and proudly. Too loudly and proudly sometimes, as though sheer volume will drown out any predemocratic hankerings. In the eighties, they surfaced anyway. The combination of Reaganomics and the Wall Street boom set off a twentieth-century version of the old nobility—Tom Wolfe's "masters of the universe." Although something was missing. What belonged to the old European nobility by right of birth only belonged to the new American one by right of money, but at least the trappings of it could be purchased.

Enter the "landed gentry" phase of new American style, spearheaded by Ralph Lauren and his faux-gentry-mansion store on upper Madison Avenue replete with winged armchairs, faded

Persian carpets, wood paneling, and manteled fireplaces, and on the dark green papered walls, silver-framed horse prints and group portraits of rowing and cricket teams. English rowing and cricket teams, of course. Evelyn Waugh's *Brideshead Revisited* may have been a big hit on American television, but the real subtext had a slightly different title: Brideshead Revered.

Close on Lauren's heels came Nell's, New York's downtown "supper club" with its canny combination of Brideshead style and Western whorehouse-saloon casualness. Spin-offs, imitations, and new angles on the same theme multiplied in those American cities that consider themselves cosmopolitan. And running beneath it all was the longing for the good old-fashioned days of Empire—for the world of movies like *A Passage to India, Maurice,* and *A Room with a View.*

In the States these movies were idolized. Cynicism was left, as it often is, to the English. Hanif Kureishi, writing in *The Guardian,* called such movies "stories of the overdressed British abroad, set against ravishing landscapes." They were romanticized escapism, he wrote, "glamorized travesties of novels by the great E. M. Forster, the sort of meaningless soft-core saccharine confection that Tory ladies and gentlemen think is Art."

That was exactly the point: Toryism—conservatism—was in. The old-fashioned kind, that is. And what a delightful contrast it was to the gritty new greed of Thatcherite Britain. Americans could hardly be blamed for denying the one and idolizing the other. As though sinking back into a feather bed of purest goose down, they abandoned themselves to nostalgia for a world they had never known. Like Henry James's Americans, they gaped at the style and ignored the sophistry.

And the English took full advantage of it. Why not? Take any English accent across the Atlantic, even a working-class one, and suddenly it's "in." An ordinary Briton becomes a wicked sophisticate somewhere in mid-flight; by the time the cab from the airport reaches town, charm and elegance float down unbidden to crown the English head.

"You must be an actress," the cab driver tells me. I've heard the line many times before, from women as well as men. He's not trying to flirt; it's the accent that does it.

His eyes examine me in the rearview mirror. "You look like Vanessa Redgrave," he says—or Maggie Smith, or Sarah Miles, my features apparently adaptable to whichever English movie he last saw.

I confess I enjoy it. It's a new sensation. In Europe, the English are considered sexlessly uninteresting. It's fun to come to the States and discover that your accent gives you dramatic allure. And it's tempting to bask in the glow of it—to smile mysteriously, don a large pair of dark glasses, and enjoy the aura of reflected glory, however naively conceived.

Many do just that. The French Riviera is no longer the playground of the Eurotrash—the coterie of descendants of long-deposed figurehead royalty clinging to defunct titles, if they are not, as rumor has it, inventing them on the cut-rate transatlantic charter. Now they flock to New York and Los Angeles, where they can dangle their titles like long feather boas, taunting and seducing the American imagination.

After all, who else will take their titles seriously?

"THE Chief Rabbi?" said the businessman in the pub near St. James's Square. "The Chief bloody Rabbi? Oh really, you're joking."

But his lunchtime drinking partner was perfectly serious. "Honest, it's true. She's gone and made the Chief Rabbi a lord."

"Good God, what's that bloody woman going to do next?"

That bloody woman—a.k.a. Margaret Thatcher—had been exercising the traditional prerogative of English prime ministers. She'd been handing out favors. Also known as titles.

Most Americans are astonished to discover that the Queen has nothing to do with the selection of those on the annual New Year's Honours List, which confers entitlement on those born unentitled. The choice of honorees is the prime minister's privilege.

Of course all the dukedoms were handed out long ago, but there are more than enough lesser ranks to go around. There's a sliding scale of entitlement, from hereditary peerages (rare) down through life peerages, knighthoods and damehoods, to the various levels of honorific in the Order of the British Empire, including CBE (Commander of the Order of the British Empire), OBE (Officer), and the mere MBE (Member). And though sometimes these titles are awarded as true honors—to scientists, actors, even to the Beatles—more often they're used to reward loyalty. Not national loyalty, but political loyalty.

This system dismays those Americans who discover its workings, many of whom had assumed that a title is the one thing money can't buy. That's why titles are so sexy in the States, even if the titled person is as poor as the proverbial English church mouse. Titles fly in the face of the American equivalence of money with status. Or so most Americans have always thought.

The English have allowed them to think that by being quite subtle about the conferring of public favors. Margaret Thatcher, however, has thrown subtlety to the winds. Captains of industry and valiant political supporters have been delighted to find that political patronage is a two-way street. Make the right political contributions, throw in a couple of choice charitable ones, and come the New Year when the Honours List is published you may reap your harvest of a title. This is the way it's done in England, and always has been. Before democracy, kings and queens did it; after democracy, prime ministers have done it in the name of the king or the queen.

The Chief Rabbi was awarded a life peerage in the 1988 list. That made him Rabbi Lord Immanuel Jakobovits for as long as he lives, but it did not suddenly change his blood from red to blue; a life peerage is not hereditary, and your eldest son cannot inherit the title. Jakobovits wasn't the first Jew to be so honored, but he was the first "professional Jew." In fact he was the first non-Anglican religious leader; though Church of England bishops are automatically elevated to the peerage, no Roman Catholic bishop has ever been so honored.

Any idea that this peerage was some sort of recognition of English Jewry was quickly squashed, not the least because of relations with the Vatican. The simple fact of the matter was that Jakobovits had been a staunchly voluble supporter of Margaret Thatcher's policies, and that elevating him to the ranks of the peerage gave Thatcher another opportunity to fly in the face of class tradition.

For good measure, she included one more controversial name on that year's list: Caspar Weinberger, the former U.S. secretary of defense. He got the honor for his support of Thatcher during her foray against Argentina over the Falklands, a war that many suspect was fought more to boost her popularity at home, by the well-tried means of chauvinism and knee-jerk patriotism, than because it was necessary.

No American had ever been knighted before. In fact, it had never even occurred to anyone that such a thing was possible. "Knight-Cap," punned the *New York Post* delightedly. The English press snorted in disgust.

At least it was only an honorary knighthood, meaning that Weinberger couldn't call himself Sir Caspar. But still, it rankled. Even those who had fully supported the Falklands War were shocked. In the clubs and pubs near St. James's Square, over the port and the pints of bitter, people wondered what the whole system of honors was coming to. A professional Jew and an American? It was unheard of. What next?

A year later, Thatcher showed them what next: She conferred an honorary knighthood on Ronald Reagan.

SHAKESPEAREAN QUAINT

THE lilacs were out in St. James's Park as I drove down The Mall and past Buckingham Palace with its usual quota of tourists peering through the railings, hoping in vain for a glimpse of royal flesh. Like most Londoners, I tend to forget that the city is a tourist mecca, so that the sudden sight of the Palace or the Tower of London or Westminster Abbey comes as an odd reminder, one that evinces a little smile of acknowledgement: "Oh yes, there it is."

I'd only be in England a few more weeks. The length of this visit hadn't affected me the way I'd anticipated. Paradoxically, the longer I stayed, the freer I felt of England—free of class, free of expectations, free of any illusion that I had to *be* English. In fact, as I rounded the Queen Victoria Memorial into Buckingham Gate, I realized that I was quite close to being a tourist myself. I felt that same curiosity and that same lack of shame about satisfying it that makes tourism enjoyable.

It had never occurred to me, the other times I'd been back, to do the things that tourists do. To be a tourist in your own country is natural in the United States, with its vast vistas and huge expanses. But in the cramped space of a European offshore island like England, it's infra dig.

Yet now, as I got caught in a traffic jam on Buckingham Palace Road, the idea of being a tourist suddenly seemed attractive. I switched on the radio to while away the time as I inched the car forward. A soft-news item featured a plug for a new musical currently being tried out at Stratford—Stephen King's *Carrie* at the Royal Shakespeare Theatre.

Stephen King? At the Royal Shakespeare Theatre? What was going on in Stratford?

Like most English people, I hadn't set foot in Stratford-upon-Avon since a compulsory school trip thirty years before. I'd never had any intention of setting foot there again, either. But in my newly discovered tourist mode it suddenly seemed a must.

Stratford, after all, is the kind of place Americans think of when they say things like, "You're so lucky, going to England." Or "It's so charming there." "So picturesque." "So quaint."

Anything in this world, of course, can be quaint. It depends on how far removed you are from it emotionally. The perception of quaintness relies on a certain distance. It only works if you can look in from the outside. And if you deny imagination.

If some place is quaint, you do not even try to imagine yourself living there, or in that way. It is safely outside you, securely distant from your own life and values and culture. In other words, you can afford to see it as quaint.

This means that by English standards, farm life in the Midwest is quaint. So is the urban sprawl of America's cities. And a McDonald's hamburger stand. Even Times Square can be quaint. The word disguises a multitude of attitudes. On what you might call the positive side there's admiration, infatuation, fantasy, nostalgia, romance; on the negative side, disdain, superiority, and a condescension not unlike that many adults still insist on adopting with young children.

Quaint says: "Look at these strange, intriguing customs of the natives."

Quaint says: "Isn't it wonderful how they manage to live this way?"

Quaint says: "How cute."

It sees the sordid transformed into the picturesque, the inconvenient made into the charming, the decaying glossed into the antique. It sees the world under a friendly sun set in a postcard-blue sky. It is blissfully and willfully ignorant of the reality of other people's lives.

No English person would ever describe England as quaint, unless, perhaps, they were being paid by the British Tourist Authority. Or unless they were engaged in one of those peculiarly English put-downs with the word *quaint* pronounced with a slight hesitation, thus making it dismissive, contemptuous, a word for a matter beneath serious consideration.

I was curious to see if Stratford would achieve quaintness for me—to test the Americanization of my eye. My English friends were quite amused by this venture, treating it as just another whim on my part. "But what on earth do you want to go there *for?"* exclaimed one.

I shrugged. "Humor me," I replied.

"So long as you don't come back raving about how quaint it all is," she said.

I set out early from London, hoping to get there and back in one day. It was pouring, but the forecast promised clearing later in the morning. On the motorway the spray from passing cars and trucks washed over my windscreen, blinding me. Everyone else was driving at seventy miles an hour, at least; I was driving at the American speed limit and I was the slowest thing on the road. In the fast lane, cars zoomed past at a hundred.

The rain had eased off by the time I reached the Midlands, but in the chill June morning with uncertain sunshine filtering through lowering clouds, Stratford was not at its picturesque best. I crossed the stone bridge over the Avon behind three tour buses and followed them through the uncomfortable mix of the sixteenth and twentieth centuries that is Stratford today. A pack of schoolchildren had clambered onto the back seat of the bus right in front of me and made faces at me as I idled along behind them. I grinned and made faces back.

I beat the tour buses to the Shakespeare Birthplace Trust on Henley Street—a modern museum built right next to the cottage where Stratford's hero was born. For four pounds and fifty pence I could gain entry to all the "Shakespeare properties"—the places where Will lived, his wife lived, his daughter lived, his mother lived, his granddaughter lived. Definitely a family business. I ran my finger down the list: Shakespeare's Birthplace, New Place, Anne Hathaway's Cottage, Mary Arden's House, Hall's Croft— all dimly remembered from that long-ago school outing when I too had piled onto the back seat of the bus to make faces at the drivers stuck behind us on the road, and the price to be paid was being dragged around all those old houses: "Single file now, no chewing gum, and no running on the stairs."

There was that memory, vague enough in itself, but super-imposed on it there was another more pervasive memory of post-cards, decorative plates, tea towels, and all manner of tourist mementos passed without consciousness in Oxford Street or Piccadilly Circus or the airport bookstore, all imprinted with the image of Anne Hathaway's Cottage, pretty and cute with its cover of honeysuckle and roses.

"You'll want to see the Hathaway Cottage of course," said the woman at the ticket counter, "but it's really worthwhile seeing everything else too, you know."

Determined to be a good tourist, I bought the whole packet. She smiled with pleasure. "An awful lot of people just want Anne Hathaway," she said. "It's the most famous one."

"Odd, seeing that it's him that wrote the plays, not her," I said.

She smiled. "They like the romance of it," she confided.

"Boy meets girl," I said.

"It always works, doesn't it?" she replied.

She insisted that I see the costume exhibit before going into the Birthplace. I really wasn't that interested, but it seemed churlish to refuse, so I allowed myself to be shepherded into a room full of big glass cases containing dummies clothed in the heavy brocaded dress of Elizabethan drama, each model labeled for a Shakespearean role: Juliet in faded pale green and gold, Othello in once-splendid purples and reds, Lady Macbeth in tired crimson.

Two Japanese girls giggled as they posed for each other's cameras in front of the costumes. They gestured to the cases and then to their own bodies, giggling all the more as they tried to imagine anyone wearing such outfits.

I could have told them what it felt like. I remembered those costumes well enough. They'd turn up the day before the annual Shakespeare production at school, hired specially for the occasion, probably from the same firm that had supplied the costumes for this exhibit. The dress rehearsal was always an awkward matter, concerned more with pins and tucks than staging and timing. Schoolgirls mouthed immortal lines while nuns knelt by their sides, lips clamped on rows of pins, pulling and tugging the stiff fabric to fit around girlish bodies until the lines became all too mortal as a pin slipped and "to be or not to be" was punctuated by a yelp of pain.

We were better out of costume than in it. The faded colors came to life in the spotlights, they assured us, but we never really believed them. Schoolgirls are suspicious of the willed suspension of disbelief. And when we put them on, the costumes seemed to stand apart from our bodies, stiff and awkward. The stiffness might have come from age, or from the sweat of too many amateur actors, or from the ornate layers of heavy brocade used for the tight bodices and bustling skirts and empty codpieces. Whichever, it transferred itself to us. Out of costume we might have been passable; in it we were farcical, and worse, we knew it.

But we did love those codpieces. As an all-girls school, we reversed the old Elizabethan practice. In Shakespeare's time, boys acted the roles of women; in ours, girls acted the roles of men.

I preferred the men's roles. I didn't have to wonder why the low-cut women's bodices revealed no appealing cleft between my breasts. Besides, with a codpiece on I could strut. I had to strut, in fact—the codpiece allowed no option—though the year I played Horatio my strut was severely impaired by constant fear of the rows of pins down either side of my tunic coming loose and pricking me in mid-sentence, adding another casualty to the orgy of onstage deaths at the end of *Hamlet*.

I left the Japanese girls taking covert close-ups of the codpieces and went out through the garden and into the house where Will was born. I'm not sure what it is about birthplaces, what attracts us to them. Surely we don't believe that bricks and stones hold some magic quality transferred by the wailing of a newborn child, yet we act as though we did. I do know that the only room I was interested in seeing was the bedroom where Will came mewling into the world. I stood and stared down at the bed—a rickety wooden affair with ropes strung across the frame in lieu of springs.

Nothing happened. No frisson of history or literature, no cultural thrill of genius in its infancy. Trying to make something of it, I decided it couldn't be "the" bed. Then I decided I was being ridiculous. Then I decided it made no difference at all where he'd been born. And decided, in the end, not to decide. It could have been any bed, any room, any house, so why not this one?

I shrugged, then regretted it. I was not playing tourist properly.

To make up for this lapse in my suspension of disbelief, I stopped in at the gift shop on my way out. Perhaps I'd find some suitable memento to put me in the mood. But the moment I walked in, all my good intentions evaporated.

Two tiny rooms were crammed with the most astonishing array of knick-knacks. There were china mugs and penny boxes printed with portraits of a very young Queen Elizabeth plus corgi (the wrong Elizabeth too—the second one, not the first). There was a tea cloth printed with the title page of the first folio edition of Shakespeare's plays, and a handwritten out-of-stock notice pinned to it. There were ashtrays printed with Anne Hathaway's Cottage and Will's Birthplace, and genteel little floral china what-nots—bells, bud vases, sugar pots, milk jugs, candlesticks—and little Wedgwood pieces made specially for the tourist trade (more bells, ashtrays, candlesticks, and so on). There were Wedgwood dinner plates with a thirty-year-old full-color photo of the Queen and Prince Philip printed on them, both young and air-brushed good-looking; they cost seventeen pounds fifty a plate. There were posters of Othello and Prospero and Malvolio all reduced to fifty pence, apparently an overrun on those three characters since no others were available at full or reduced price. There was lots of Peter Rabbit bath seed and soap and figurines and china. Lots. There was more Beatrix Potter, in fact, than Shakespeare. "It's for our younger visitors," said one of the sales-women, smiling. The only line that could compete with Beatrix for sheer volume was Crabtree & Evelyn—sachets, potpourri, jams, sauces, chutneys piled up in cute wicker baskets.

I had found the heart of quaintness.

It reminded me of one of those gift shops on American highways—the ones next door to the rest rooms and the soda machines, right opposite the entrance to the Burger King. With one major difference: The American highway gift shops had no pretensions to good taste. They weren't trying to piggyback on Shakespeare or any other culture, not even the culture of the American road. They were unashamedly, unabashedly, collections of kitsch, intended as the last resort of those who'd forgotten to buy a present for their nieces or nephews, for guilty salesmen arriving home suspiciously late, or for harried parents trying to buy peace in the back seat.

There's a wonderful Yiddish word, *tchatchkes,* for all sorts of decorative bits and pieces which you never need but which some-how tend to accumulate around you, mainly as a result of the kind of well-intentioned little gifts you are given as tokens. Tchatchkes are a subspecies of kitsch. It seemed a perfect irony that only Yiddish could do justice to the gift shop in Shakespeare's Birthplace. I wondered if Will would have appreciated that.

Certainly the English would not. American kitsch has become a flamboyant celebration of total tastelessness, so much so that items such as outrageously shaped diners—a hamburger or a dinosaur or a castle—have become an art form, tastelessness elevated into taste as Americans celebrate their ability to create outrageous ghastliness. Kitsch, in other words, has become fun. But the kind of English kitsch that goes by the name of quaintness is relentlessly serious. The knick-knacks in the Shakespeare gift store were created in the service of a rigid conception of what constitutes good taste, lifeless and joyless.

Will, with his raunchy sense of humor and outrageous puns, would have loved American kitsch. He'd have fled in horror from all these tasteful knick-knacks. I imagined him rolling in his grave and decided to find it by the end of the day, just to check.

CLEARLY I was not yet American enough to be awed or entranced by either quaintness or age.

American tourists look at the physical remains of their own history—the simple forts, the picket fences—and yearn for the grandeur of solid, ornate stone, taking literally the old saw that an Englishman's home is his castle. They idolize Castle Howard, the mansion that played the star role in the television version of Evelyn Waugh's *Brideshead Revisited.* They buy Burberry raincoats when a real live hereditary lord models them; they buy Schweppes soda when another hereditary lord urges them to do so. They are blissfully unaware of the lack of dignity in peddling raincoats and soda, just as they are unaware of the fact that one man's castle may be another man's albatross—a burden of debts and repairs, leaking roofs and rusting gutters, dry rot and wet rot and woodworm and the thousand other ailments that attack buildings that have outlived their function.

These lords are part of the new England—an England living on its past. The English are developing their tourist trade as fast as they can, museumizing their older towns and flogging the old, the cute, and the traditional to death. Perhaps familiarity with the past breeds a certain contempt for it.

I felt stifled after the gift shop. I needed to walk. Back out on the street, I took a deep breath. The sky was low and gray but the smell of rain was still faint and I decided to make straight for the Hathaway cottage, a mile or so out of town. At least, in Will's days it was out of town. The footpath I now followed led past the backyards of row houses and then through school playing fields. The architecture was modern drab, but it was a relief to be away from all those half-timbered Elizabethan houses; even the hockey fields of the local comprehensive school seemed refreshingly open and free.

Not far from the cottage, I passed a row of tiny one-up, one-down fifteenth-century houses. Tavern Row, said the street sign. I looked for the tavern, but it seemed to be long gone. Perhaps it had been there in Will's time. In fact, I decided, that must have been what brought him here: He came for his quaff of ale, walking across the fields to escape the properness of Stratford, and then one afternoon, drunkenly walking the wrong way, he'd bumped into Anne by the stream, and the rest is history, or at least myth.

Well, and why not? It made more sense than the image of Will presenting himself hat in hand at the front door of the cottage. Or perhaps I only found that so hard to imagine because the Hathaway cottage was so very like my parents' one in Berkshire.

I'd hated that cottage when they first moved into it a year after I'd left home for university. After the huge, roomy mansion I'd grown up in with its oak-paneled reception rooms and long flagstoned terrace and wide windowsills—wide enough for a child to curl up on with a book—the cottage seemed horribly poky. In fact it was roomy for its time. It was an early sixteenth-century house, built just ten years after the Hathaway one, and like that one, roofed with Norfolk-reed thatch. It had all the details of age: the well in the garden, ornate but long dry; the four-hundred-year-old apple tree which had bent over, touched the ground, rerooted itself, and still bore apples—hard, bitter little things, like all fruits of history, perhaps; the sloping floors that creaked and groaned under the weight of even the slimmest human being; the low beams that caught your forehead with a sickening crack until you learned to duck; the drafts around the lead-paned windows, through the beams, under the doors; the constant battle against birds nesting in the thatch; the antiquated plumbing that had remained stubbornly problematic through successive attempts at modernization . . .

It only became a pleasure to visit once I'd left England, when my eyes became foreign and the cottage became—yes, quaint.

The Hathaway place was not in as good shape as my parents'. Old houses need to be lived in. When they become museums, they lose the humanity that comes from people's lives. They get damp and stiff, like old bones in an English winter. Maybe you don't notice it when the roses and the honeysuckle are in bloom and the sun is shining, but on this chill day neither were yet in bloom and the sky remained persistently dark.

Inside there was the same smell of scented wood polish that had pervaded Will's Birthplace, the same echoing emptiness, and on the way out, the same gift-shop minefield of quaint souvenirs with Beatrix Potter in the ascendancy. At least I was lucky in one respect; impeccable timing had seen me through the cottage ahead of one tour bus and behind another. In the parking lot I watched the new batch of tourists pouring out of the bus, and wondered why they so easily allowed themselves to be guided and shepherded everywhere. For me, the point of tourism was in the freedom to wander, not in the scheduled presentation of predetermined sights.

So wander I did, heading slowly back into town and feeling like Will might have done if he'd walked all that way and found

Anne not at home. I decided to do what he would have done—drown my sorrows in a quaff of ale.

I made for The Dirty Duck. That was the pub where the actors from the nearby Royal Shakespeare Theatre drank, I'd been told. It wasn't as old as Shakespeare, but it might be the closest in atmosphere to his time. Besides, it was down by the river.

Avon, sweet Avon—a polite little river with the requisite number of ducks and weeping willows, and until not long ago plenty of swans too. I saw lots of ducks all right, but no swans. They're fast becoming a rarity in England, victims to the lead in anglers' weights. Some years back, in ironic response to the changing bird scene on the Avon, the actors dubbed The Black Swan pub "The Dirty Duck." The name stuck; now one side of the old sign still hanging from the upper floor shows the swan, and the other, the duck.

It was pleasant enough, and I ate a steak-and-kidney pie to go with a couple of pints of bitter as I looked over the actors and they looked over me and the Avon went flowing past the window. But I knew that Will would never have quaffed his ale here—it was far too "nice." The Crack in Liverpool would have been his kind of tavern, but that kind of place doesn't exist in small towns. No wonder he left for London.

An elderly couple asked permission to sit opposite me in the window seat. They'd driven over from Kenilworth, they said, for a spot of lunch. "Why Stratford?" I asked. "That sounds, if you'll forgive the analogy, like coals to Newcastle."

They both smiled. "It's just so pleasant here by the river," she replied.

"When you can avoid the tourists," he added by way of clarification. "You can't even sit in this pub on a sunny day; in fact you can hardly see the river for all the tour buses going by. Jerries, Japs, Yanks . . ."

His wife's leg seemed to move suddenly under the table. He reddened slightly.

"Very good tourists too, the Americans," he added quickly. "Our daughter was there last year. She went to New York and then to Miami. Had a wonderful time. Where are you from over there?"

So I quaffed my ale, taken for an American and perhaps rightly so, and talked of New York as I stared out at the Avon and wondered why all famous rivers always seem to flow upstream. Was it a trick of the wind, or of physics, or of the ale? It was time to consult with Will.

I took my leave and set off drunkenly along the river to Holy Trinity Church where Will is buried. Halfway there, the heavens did what they'd been threatening to do all morning: They opened, and I got drenched. Wet inside and out, to the head-shaking amusement of the church warden, I paid my entrance fee and wandered up the aisle, leaving a trail of water on the huge stone slabs of the floor.

Like most English churches, it was a mix of centuries. The fine carved wooden roof was eighteenth century. The choir stalls were fifteenth century. The little store by the church entrance was very much twentieth century. The graves set into the steps leading to the altar were seventeenth century; they were almost indistinguishable from ordinary flagstones except they were larger and engraved.

Will's was slightly off to the left, beside Anne's. He died in 1616, at age fifty-two, and on his grave were the words he ordered:

> *Good friend for Jesus' sake forbeare*
> *To dig the dust encloased here!*
> *Blessed be the man that spares thes stones*
> *And curst be hye that moves my bones.*

Will growled at me from the grave. I smiled. He probably wrote those lines of an evening in an earthy, filthy, noisy tavern somewhere in London, with a grin on his face and a beer mug in his hand.

I turned my back on the dust enclosed there and caught the eye of one of the gargoyles carved into the choir stalls, mockingly sticking its tongue out at me.

Shakespeare had chosen his burial place well. That gargoyle was surely his prescient comment on all that had happened to Stratford in his name.

"Right on, Will," I thought, "you've got it." And walked out in the happily drunken assurance that Shakespeare could tolerate quaintness no better than I.

JULY FOURTH

SUMMER finally arrived, and with it the extraordinary seductiveness of English summer evenings.

The light begins to change at about six. It gentles the urban landscape and spreads a soft, almost dreamlike mantle over the rural one. As it gradually fades—so gradually it's almost imperceptible—the dying sun plays off the clouds, creating long sunsets. At the height of summer, darkness comes only close to ten o'clock. These evening hours of soft light seem like a gift, a time in which whatever happens has an almost magical quality, set apart from real life.

Romances begin in these hours of fading light. People stroll by the rivers, sit comfortably outside the pubs, wander into the parks and smell the drifting scent of new-mown grass—that special grass of England, soft and fine, so unlike the coarser American species. It's the grass that makes the famous English lawns, and that sometimes, if you walk barefoot, can feel like moss beneath your skin.

In this evening light on village greens and in city parks, cricketers appear, all dressed in white. Casual, slow, relaxing, cricket is the perfect game to gather people together. Afterwards players and onlookers retire to the nearest pub to consolidate the camaraderie of evening.

In London's Regent's Park the dying light gentles the stone of the Nash terraces surrounding it, making them seem like stage sets for a ballet. Clouds gather high in the sky as the city cools, and change color as the sun shifts, lowering. Groups gather here after work, pace out their playing fields on the lawns, and take practice swings as the order of play is established. Bat cracks against ball. Murmurs go up in polite English tones: "Nicely played." "Well fielded." "Home run!"

Home run?

It's a long summer evening in Regent's Park and I'm suffering from cultural dislocation. This isn't cricket we're playing; this is softball. The all-American game under a Turner sky. The well-oiled willow of the cricket bat transformed into the aluminum tube of softball. Wickets replaced by bases. Bare hands smothered in the huge appendage of the baseball glove.

In the distance, other teams are playing the same game. They're company teams—film production companies, public relations companies, advertising agencies—the kind of service firms that have grouped in the Camden Town area, just north of Regent's Park.

I'm playing with a team of architects against a team of designers. By the time we finish, the score will be 30-30, an outcome evidently satisfactory to all concerned, as nobody will even suggest extra innings. There's not an American on the field except for me, half-American, half-English, wondering why, all of a sudden, the English have discovered baseball.

What did it was television. Channel 4 television, to be specific. In the early eighties the upstart new channel realized that it needed to broadcast sports if it was to develop a wider audience. But tennis, golf, racing, snooker, soccer, cricket, and the Olympics were all monopolized by the BBC and ITV. The new channel's only hope of making it against such well-entrenched competition was to be daring, innovative, and somewhat outrageous. So it came up with a daring, innovative, and somewhat outrageous solution: America.

Enter onto British screens American football and baseball. At first it seemed a stroke of desperation. What self-respecting Briton was going to waste time watching American sports? The answer was no self-respecting Briton, of course, but the young and the restless, whose locus of self-respect was far away, over the Atlantic.

By the late eighties English fans were complaining that the commentators were talking down to them, assuming they didn't know the games. The director of Channel 4, Jeremy Isaacs, had gained a reputation for genius for his daring decision. Baseball and football paraphernalia were seen in stores and on the streets, charter planes were flying off for the Super Bowl and the World Series, a slew of books explaining baseball and football hit the stores—and I was playing softball in Regent's Park.

The cultural dislocation was all the stronger since the last ball field I'd been on was the old Huggins-Stengel field in Saint Petersburg, Florida, where I'd covered the New York Mets in spring training just before leaving for this visit to England. It was the last spring the Mets would spend there before moving to their spanking new complex at Port Saint Lucie on the other side of the Florida peninsula.

Sitting on the locker-room steps in the Florida sunshine, chewing tobacco and talking with the guys, I was the only journalist around. I thought I was in baseball heaven.

Occasionally the cry "Heads up!" would be heard, and like everyone else I'd look up. Unlike everyone else, I couldn't see a thing. Eventually I stopped looking, and when the ball came veering down three feet from my head and I hadn't budged, the Mets stared at me with respect for my guts, not suspecting, with their sharp eyes, that I simply hadn't seen it. I didn't disillusion them.

I talked the Zen of baseball with Ron Darling and Bobby Ojeda. I stuffed myself with locker-room doughnuts and coffee with Roger McDowell and Sid Fernandez. I stood behind home plate with Davey Johnson and Joe McIlvaine and listened as they analyzed Doc Gooden's performance, pitch by pitch. Baseball, I thought, didn't get any better than this.

But then I'd never played it. That particular pleasure was reserved for Regent's Park. I'd had to come all the way back to England to discover the exhilaration of getting a hit, of sliding into base, of catching a fly ball on the run. And that was eight years after I'd first discovered the game.

Baseball was part of my psychological immigration to the States. From the beginning, I grasped that it was an integral part of the American psyche. To know baseball was to proclaim yourself American, to enter the realm of American mythology, to ally yourself with the very essence of Americanness. And of the American language.

This became crystal clear to me after my first baseball game—a many-splendored memory, as the first game surely is for nearly all Americans. It was only my second day in the States, but New York friends, shocked that I had never even seen a diamond, had hustled me off to Yankee Stadium. Where, among the other splendors, I witnessed for the first time the American language being acted out.

Though I knew no Americans when I lived in England, since those were the years when America was still considered a brash black sheep of the English-speaking family and was not mentioned in polite society, I came to know many in the years I lived in Israel. And since they were the only people with whom I spoke English, I picked up their language. I could touch base, give a ballpark figure, strike out, and reach first base long before I ever realized that these were baseball terms. I could be out of the ball game, let alone out of the ballpark. I could play ball—even hardball when I had to. There were times when I climbed the walls, and accused others of being off the wall. And it seemed I had a talent for throwing the occasional curveball in an argument.

I never stopped to wonder why these expatriate Americans were so obsessed with bases and balls. Without realizing it, I was reveling in the vigor of the American language, which despite certain evidence to the contrary is not at all the same as the British language. For some reason Americans—academic Americans in particular—seem to be rather ashamed of this, admiring what they evidently consider the sophisticated superiority of British English. But as the British would say, I beg to differ.

American English is not as devilishly polite as the British version. It has vitality. It has guts. You can swear much better in American. You can yell and raise hell and raise dust and raise the dead. You can change and invent and bend and play with the language. Where British English is a slow-pitch softball, American English is a major-league spitball, breaking the rules and charting its own unruly course from mound to strike zone. It is a boisterous language with a life of its own. And not long ago it took the pennant. No less an authority than one Dr. Robert Burchfield, editor of the fourth and final volume of the supplement to the twelve-volume *Oxford English Dictionary*—the definitive guide to English as she should be spoke—confessed that when it came to the evolution of the language, "America is leading the way now, not Britain."

MY Americanization began with language. Slowly, inexorably, over the years I lived in Jerusalem my language became American. And I grasped not only the language itself, but also the culture that spawned it.

Partly, this came from the movies. There were a dozen movie houses in Jerusalem; of them, ten were showing American movies at any one time. But that was a passive acceptance of the language; what really changed me was my active adoption of it.

In 1973, I began to work in Time-Life's Jerusalem bureau, reporting for *Time* magazine and Time-Life Books. Time-Life did not suffer from Anglophilia; the request quickly came down to write American style, instead of British. I had no objection, but quickly discovered that this was a somewhat more complex matter than I'd imagined. It was not just a matter of spelling, of dropping a "u" in a word like "ardour" or transposing the last letters of a word like "theatre." The grammar was different too, and the phrasing of the sentences. At first I had to concentrate, scanning everything I wrote for its "Americanness." But after a while it began to feel natural, and after another while English phrasing began to feel forced and stilted. American phrasing was freer. It allowed more leeway. It was more fun.

I didn't realize it at the time, but I began to deliberately seek out American writing. I read *Time* or *Newsweek* the same way people in the Midwest read them—to plug into what was happening in the cultural and political centers of the East and West coasts. I borrowed American classics from the expatriates I knew, and the latest issues of American magazines. Visiting England, I'd look for American authors on the paperback racks. English authors were entertaining, to be sure, and sometimes very elegant. I knew of no American writing to match the elegance of an Anthony Burgess or a Lawrence Durrell. But American authors seemed to have a vitality, a nowness, that the English lacked, and I reveled in it.

By the time I arrived in the States, I had read more American literature than most American literature graduates. I'd read Faulkner and Hemingway and Steinbeck and F. Scott Fitzgerald. I'd read Hawthorne and Dreiser and Nathanael West. I'd read Kerouac and Corso and Ginsberg and Ferlinghetti, and Miller and Styron and Roth and Mailer. Much of it I reread in the years to follow, and realized how much I'd missed that first time around when I hadn't been able to read all the cultural signposts. But much of it I grasped, not only in its universal meaning but also in its particular American detail, and this American detail became part of my life too, part of my own system of cultural reference, even though I'd never set foot in the States.

My geographical reference widened as well. Americans in Jerusalem introduced me to the cultural meaning of Dubuque,

Iowa or Newark, New Jersey, to the subtle shadings between L.A. and San Francisco, or between Boston, New York, and Washington. I knew the spirit of these places long before I had any real idea of what they looked like.

And when I finally arrived in the States things looked surprisingly as I had expected. Those writers wrote well, and the moviemakers had done their jobs. New York—the skyscrapers, Central Park, the Bowery, Fifth Avenue, the Village, even Wall Street—all came for me as confirmation rather than surprise.

All, that is, except for Times Square. Nothing had primed me for Times Square. I was not prepared for a mere "X" instead of what I thought of as a real square—a London square like Grosvenor Square where my appointment with my American Samarra was to take place many years later. And I was certainly not prepared for the sheer grunginess of it: the Third World rundown atmosphere and the insulting sordidness of the porno parlors and the fake cut-rate stores and the general sense of threat that pervaded those few blocks of Broadway and Seventh Avenue. They never show all this in the movies.

With that one exception, however, I took what I knew for granted. Until one night at a dinner party, when I made some comment. I've forgotten the subject; it might have been Watergate, or the quality of life in Seattle, or what still seems to me the very American phenomenon of the occasional quiet madman who suddenly erupts into fury and opens fire in public, mowing down strangers. Whichever, the comment struck the man seated to my right as odd, coming from me.

"How come you know so much about America?" he asked suspiciously. "I thought you said you'd only been here a few weeks."

"I didn't know I knew that much," I replied.

"You talk as though you'd lived here for years. You know all the points of reference."

"It must be from films," I said, deliberately using the English word to reassure him of my foreignness. I was both pleased and bemused. Until that point I'd had no idea how much I knew of America.

It is often difficult for Americans to grasp that foreigners know far more about them than they do about other countries. I had the foreigner's knowledge of the States that comes from what anti-Americans call "cultural imperialism"—the worldwide reach of American popular culture, which may be symbolized by Coca-Cola, hamburgers, and blue jeans, but goes far deeper than that. American fantasies become the world's fantasies. "Dynasty" is seen all over the world, kids play cowboys and astronauts no matter where they are, and throughout the Eastern bloc and the Third World, American cigarettes, cars, jeans, and music are admired and bartered as status symbols.

"Cultural imperialism" is just the surface of the worldwide influence and importance of a superpower. I had been living in a country that was halfway around the world from the States, yet heavily dependent on it. Israel received larger American loans and aid than any other country; not surprisingly, news coverage of things American was extensive. The nightly television newscast out of Jerusalem would often give more time to what had happened that day in Washington than I was to find later on the twenty-two-minute network newscasts in the States. Living in Israel, I knew how American government worked and how American elections were run. I had detailed information on the fluctuating relationships between the White House, the Department of State, and the Pentagon. None of this was consciously learned—it was all simply information that impinged on my existence as a reasonably intelligent and political being living in Jerusalem.

And if I had been living in London? I might have known somewhat less because the political situation is not as immediately compelling, but in London too, knowledge of America has become vitally important. Fond memories of the days Britannia ruled the waves have finally been put aside and a new realism acknowledges that Britain has ceded world power and influence to the States. With Europe physically in the middle of a potential superpower conflagration, and American missile bases on European soil, London is now as concerned with what happens in Washington—and how it happens—as all other world capitals.

All over the world people read America, literally and figuratively. And in England, which had maintained a snobbish disdain of all things American through the sixties, a new inverse snobbery has come into being. If America was once seen as all crassness and vulgarity, now that crassness has been transformed in English eyes into honesty, and the vulgarity into vitality. American Anglophilia is being reciprocated in a way calculated to rock and shock the basis of the Anglophile's world. The English, you see, are becoming Americaphiles.

AMERICAPHILIA raises its tricolored head everywhere you look in England nowadays. On television, for instance, the most popular programs are American imports: "Cagney and Lacey," "Dynasty," "Dallas," "Hill Street Blues," "Kate and Allie," "L.A. Law," "Cheers." The English follow them with the same fascination as Americans following the English sagas of public television's "Masterpiece Theatre" series. "The American shows deal with real life," English fans say, "real problems. Who needs all those historic soap operas? The Americans react to whatever's happening right now."

The West End, London's center stage, has also succumbed, discovering the vulgar delights of the American musical. *Guys and Dolls* made a nice change from Ibsen at the National Theatre, even as Broadway was reeling under a virtual invasion of British imports.

The English are even reading American books. When I was studying English literature in school, the curriculum was very literal: This was *English* literature, and so far as the curriculum setters were concerned, the Americans didn't have such a thing as literature. But now, despite the annual hoopla over the Booker Prize, the locus of contemporary English literature has shifted from one side of the Atlantic to the other. As one top English editor said over an old-fashioned publisher's lunch, "We're really little more than a reprint industry for American books nowadays."

And as for the transatlantic airlines, they're gleefully raking it in. Twenty years ago—even ten—a trip to the United States was considered a grand irrelevance by most English people. But nowadays to have visited America is a sign of sophistication, just like a visit to England for most Americans. And this new familiarity has bred not contempt—that came from ignorance—but envy and admiration. It's as though to be American is somehow more real than to be English. More in touch with the world. More alive.

"Even American holidays are more fun," said the friends who invited me to a July Fourth concert on Hampstead Heath.

In the States it would have been considered a perfect July Fourth—sunny and warm, a gentle breeze, a few small fluffy clouds floating high on a deep blue sky. From the heights of Hampstead Heath there was a splendid view over the whole of London: the spires, steeples, and domes of the old churches and abbeys and cathedrals, and the stark geometric forms of the new high-rise cathedrals—the corporate headquarters in the City.

Not many years ago I'd hardly have known it was July Fourth. Not in London. The date was as innocuously meaningless as most of the other days in the year, with about the same value as Christmas Day in Iraq or Bastille Day in China. But now there was no avoiding it. All day the main light music station of the BBC, Radio Two, had been playing American theme music. The deejay had a south London accent but the words and phrases he was using were American.

No doubt expatriate Americans were having barbecues somewhere in London, but the English didn't yet know about that particular tradition. Instead, we were heading for a picnic and open-air concert, one of a regular series of free concerts organized by English Heritage, the umbrella organization for the National Trust.

"But how can English Heritage be having a July Fourth concert?" I asked. "Isn't it against their principles or something?"

My friends shrugged. "Isn't that what Americans do on July Fourth?" they said. "Have fun?"

"Yes, of course, but English Heritage celebrating American Independence Day seems rather like American Heritage celebrating the Queen's birthday."

"Things have changed," my friends said. "We like America now."

I was feeling vaguely disoriented as we parked the car and began walking across the Heath, carrying blankets and picnic hampers. There'd be tall ships sailing in New York Harbor, I thought. And red, white, and blue fireworks. And fireboats spurting colored columns of water under the Brooklyn Bridge.

We made for the sloping grassy natural amphitheater at Kenwood, the big mansion at the top of the Heath. At the bottom of the slope was a small lake, and on an island in the lake, a band shell with chairs and instruments ready for the appearance of the London Symphony Orchestra. I'd expected to hear a steady stream of American accents as we walked across the slope looking for a good picnic site, but the overwhelming majority of the voices were English. A couple wandered by wrapped in American flags. They were both English. Some people played frisbee on the big lawn with children and dogs. They were English too.

Picnics were laid out. Champagne bottles were opened for adults, Coca-Cola bottles for kids. The crowd packed the fenced-in concert area and overflowed onto the open lawn. We found a good spot, laid down our blankets, and started in on our supper, fielding a stray frisbee here and there as we ate. By the time the orchestra came out onto the band shell, they had a very receptive audience.

The program was made to order for the occasion: lots of Sousa, Gershwin, and Bernstein, music so familiar and yet so alien in this setting. There was "Rhapsody in Blue," and excerpts from *West Side Story*, then fireworks exploded high above the lake as the orchestra launched with gusto into "The Stars and Stripes Forever." The audience sang along happily, using the words of the football stadium chant: "Here we go, here we go, here we go . . ."

I sang too, suddenly comfortable in this musical confusion of nationality. And as I sang, I remembered a Sunday morning some years before in the small town of Bennington, New Hampshire.

There had been a sale going on in the town library, opposite the church, and I'd been going through a pile of books in the vestibule as the two librarians, gray-haired rosy-cheeked New England ladies, watched carefully to make sure this stranger from out of town didn't "borrow" anything.

I was looking through a tattered farmer's almanac from three years before when the church bells began to peal. It took a moment for me to realize that they were pealing a tune. The tune was "God Save the Queen."

I did an aural double take. "Excuse me," I said, "but why are your church bells ringing 'God Save the Queen'?"

They looked at me in astonishment. "But that's 'My Country 'Tis of Thee,' " they said.

I'd heard of the song, but lacking an American childhood, I'd never heard it sung. "It is?" I said.

"Oh yes," they replied. And taking pity on an ignorant foreigner, the two of them stood ramrod straight and waveringly but proudly sang the words along with the church bells.

Listening to them in that place, it wasn't hard to flip back two, three, four hundred years, to a time when others had fled England for America. They brought their tunes with them, and simply wrote new words. An English tune, American words—

familiar yet alien music. But then that, I thought, is what America does: It allows you to write your own words to the old familiar tunes. You may be English, but through words, you can become American.

GREEN CARD

MAYFAIR is the highest priced property on the English Monopoly board, which like Monopoly boards everywhere is hopelessly out of date. Any area so subject to Americanization—with the American Embassy, the Hilton, and the Playboy Club all within a few minutes' walk—was bound to suffer a certain decline in reputation, though certainly not in price. Mayfair has long since bowed to Belgravia for reclusively moneyed elegance but it still houses some of London's oldest and shabbiest gentlemen's clubs, and still draws the tourists convinced that this is the true heart of London.

The American Embassy on Grosvenor Square is not one of London's more attractive buildings. The massive concrete facade dominates the whole of the west side of the square and there were choruses of protest in 1960 when it was built. In one of those Virginia suburbs close to Washington D.C. it would probably have been considered quite elegant. Or in Saint Louis where Eero Saarinen, the architect, had designed the controversial Gateway Arch. But alongside the old elegance of Mayfair's Georgian townhouses and mansions, the embassy has the same effect as a broad Midwestern accent booming through the hush of one of those exclusive clubs.

Nevertheless, it is impressive. It was designed to impress. Built in the style of defensible architecture—a science in itself—it even has a moat around it.

That moat is puzzling. Perhaps Saarinen was thinking of an Englishman's home as his castle, and imagined he could provide a modern counterpart to the moated country castles of the titled gentry. Or perhaps he had visions of hordes of rioting Britons assaulting his embassy, to be repelled by brave Marines manning the ramparts in a role reversal of Gordon at Khartoum or an Anglicized version of Custer's last stand.

In fact, it's the kind of embassy that would have made sense in Iran. In retrospect, it seems quite possible that some State Department planner made a mistake back there in the sixties—put the wrong plans in the wrong envelopes, as it were. If it had been built in Teheran, the hostage crisis might never have taken place.

As happens at American embassies and consulates everywhere in the world (except for the Soviet bloc, and that is not for lack of wishing), lines form outside the embassy in Grosvenor Square. There is a certain look in the eyes of those who line up outside American embassies, whether in England, Mexico, or South Korea. A certain way of standing. A certain attitude that fills the air and hovers over the line like a small cloud. It is the look of the supplicant—bowed, patient, afraid to step out of line, literally or metaphorically, lest the chances of success be somehow arbitrarily ruined by fate, some unknown rule, or the whim of whatever visa official is fulfilling the role of The Powers That Be on that particular day.

That line had been there one mild, sunny spring morning some years before, when on a trip to England I'd gone to the embassy to renew my American visa—an annual ritual for "temporary working aliens" such as myself. People were lined up in very orderly fashion all the way down the broad flight of steps at the embassy's side entrance on Upper Grosvenor Street. It was definitely an English line—a queue. Nobody crowded anyone else, and they had arranged themselves along the very side of the steps, hugging the parapet over the moat as though each person was pretending that he or she was not really there—as though they could fade into the stone and become the epitome of inconspicuousness.

I joined the end of the line and looked longingly over at the broad expanse of the steps, most of which was in the sun. Only the edge of the steps, where the line had formed, was in the shade.

"Seems crazy to be standing here in the shade, doesn't it?" I said to the man in front of me.

He glanced round at me and grunted slightly, then turned away again. The look on his face was one of strained patience with people who talk to themselves when standing on line.

"It looks so nice there in the sun," I said, undaunted.

He flashed a tight, embarrassed smile, like a New Yorker trying to get past a panhandler on the street.

"Tell you what," I said, "if I go sit there, can you keep my place in line for me?"

He looked vague, whether out of discomfort or annoyance was hard to tell, but finally came out with a grudging "All right."

I flashed him a big smile, which he ignored.

I moved across the steps and settled down in the sunshine about five or six steps down from the top, well above the exhaust of the cabs speeding off Grosvenor Square and along Upper Grosvenor Street. New York cabs may be dangerous by virtue, if that is the right word, of bad driving, but London cabs are dangerous by design. London cabbies have no patience for errant pedestrians setting foot on their turf, the street. Rather than slow down for a pedestrian, they'll speed up and make straight for the interloper. It was good to be sitting safely above them.

The sun was even gaining some warmth. I blinked in the unaccustomed sunlight, put my purse down beside me and began to check out the front page of my newspaper. All I needed was a styrofoam cup of coffee and I could have been on the steps of New York's Forty-second Street Library or Metropolitan Museum—except that nobody else was sitting there and there was no mime to entertain me.

Occasionally I'd look over at the line to see if it was moving. It wasn't. Each time I looked, it seemed longer. Soon it reached the bottom of the steps and continued on around the railings of the moat on the inside edge of the pavement. I caught a few strange looks—faces averted the moment they realized I'd seen them looking—and remembered that in England people did not sit on steps, even in the sunshine.

I shrugged. If they wanted to shiver on their feet in the shade, so be it. The day was far too nice to worry about behaving in an appropriately English manner. Besides, this was the American Embassy.

I settled into the newspaper. I'd bought the *International Herald Tribune* that morning so I could check out the baseball scores. The Mets weren't doing so well without me there to scream encouragement at the television set.

The Mets . . . I was off in a reverie about Mookie Wilson at bat and the roar of the crowd and a looping single to right just where it was needed, when I heard a small commotion behind me at the top of the steps. I turned to look up and saw a young mother backing out of the revolving doors, maneuvering a toddler's pushchair. She looked hot and bothered as only the English do in the sun. She had long straggly blond hair, a rumpled cotton frock, and a fringed tapestry shoulder bag that was caught in the revolving doors. The toddler hung on to his mother's left hand as she struggled with the door; the bag came free, and then the carriage stuck. Her other child, a small boy about six years old, had already made it through. He watched impassively, hugging a brightly colored rubber ball.

The mother was flustered and angry. "You stay where you are, you hear me?" she shouted at the boy. Sure enough, an English accent. Perhaps she'd just been denied a visa.

I looked over at the people on line. Everyone was conscientiously looking elsewhere. The English may have a reputation for being polite, but that does not necessarily mean helpful. I was about to get up and help her when the carriage suddenly came free of the door. She bent down and began to rearrange its contents.

I shrugged and turned to the front page of the *Trib.* Time to find out what was happening in the world. I was minding my own and Ronald Reagan's business when some thirty seconds later the rubber ball came bouncing past me down the steps, picking up speed as it went. Red, yellow, and blue flashed in quick succession. Bounce, bounce, bounce, every two or three steps, a little colored ball of anarchy heading for the sidewalk and the street.

"So much for that rubber ball," I thought, and went back to the front page, only half aware of the fact that behind me, the little boy had begun to bounce down the steps after his ball, determined to retrieve it before it got squashed beneath the wheels of one of the cabs speeding in off the square.

He bounced right by me. I glanced up. He was going pretty fast. And then everything seemed to happen in slow motion.

I looked at the people on line. They were all watching the boy with the impassive look of disinterested observers. The English are so good at that look. Nobody seemed about to move. I looked up at the mother. She was fussing with the carriage, trying to get it open and obviously unaware of what was happening. I looked down at the ball, which was in the street by now, a multicolored flash bouncing around from one taxicab wheel to another. And slowly, horribly slowly, I saw what was going to happen.

The slow motion broke into rapid action and I was down the steps, over the sidewalk, into the street, and practically under a taxicab myself as I snatched the boy out of the cab's way and deposited him back on the sidewalk.

For a moment the boy was too stunned to react. Another cab caught the ball and it split with a pop, ruptured into a sorry shred of rubber splayed on the asphalt. He stared at it, drew breath, and burst out into a long, loud, bawling cry. I heard his mother yell in response.

Dragging toddler and carriage, she lumbered down the steps,

grabbed the boy, and smacked him across the face. He took another deep breath of shock and dismay and resumed his bawling louder than ever. She pushed the toddler into the carriage, straightened the boy's jacket, grabbed his hand, and firmly dragged him off, crying and kicking. She hadn't even looked at me, let alone said a word.

I stood there on the sidewalk and watched her retreat. The boy's crying was soon drowned out by the noise of the traffic. I looked over at the people on line. Nobody had moved. The moment they saw me looking, they all turned away, clearly embarrassed at having been caught in the act. "Stop staring," I heard an internal voice say across the years. "It's not polite to stare."

I shrugged, went back up the steps to where my purse and newspaper lay, and sat down again. The sun was warm. The cabs whizzed by down below. The line had still not moved. Everything was exactly the same as before. It was as though nothing at all had happened.

For a moment I wondered if anything *had* really happened. Maybe I'd just been having a little fugue, a minor seizure induced by boredom. But no—my heart was still beating fast from the sudden spurt down the steps and into the street. I took note of my heartbeat with a certain gratitude; if it hadn't been for that, I could have sworn right then that the whole incident had taken place solely in my imagination.

I picked up the newspaper but my hands were shaking from adrenalin and I couldn't read. I looked over at the people on line again. They were all ostentatiously looking the other way, at the blank wall of the embassy. I wondered how long they would have stood there and just watched the little boy. If I hadn't moved when I did, how long would it have been until someone had broken rank with the deeply inculcated English habit of "Don't interfere," and done something? Would they have moved in time?

I shivered in the sun. Would they have moved at all?

If these had been those other New York steps, there'd have been dozens of people dashing for the street. A crowd would have gathered around. Everybody would have had something to say. About taxicabs speeding. About giving kids rubber balls to play with in the street. About bringing kids up in the city. About anything at all—any excuse to break down the anonymity of the city and talk, get involved, feel for a moment like a real person in the street. The boy would have been patted and hugged, scolded and reassured. Someone would have given him candy, perhaps. And everyone—everyone within sight—would have been smiling.

When the visa line finally began to move, it moved quickly. I resumed my former place in it and thanked the man in front of me for keeping it.

"Nice day to sit in the sun," he said. And that was all. I knew he'd seen what had happened, but he made no reference to it. Not even "nice work," or "nice move." Just a nice day to sit in the sun.

"Well, to hell with him," I thought, but smiled nonetheless. After all, how often do you get to save a little boy's life?

IT had all seemed very auspicious then, and my visa had been renewed on the spot. But now, years later, the day of my immigration interview dawned dark and rainy. It was the kind of hard English rain that soaks you straight through, and that settles in for a day at a time. The kind of rain that puts everyone in a bad mood.

I found a parking garage that still had space off South Audley Street, some three hundred yards away from Grosvenor Square. Under an awning on the street, I contemplated the inevitable mad dash through the rain to the embassy. Cabs sped by, throwing huge sheets of spray onto my skirt. All of them were full. Same as New York—never an empty cab in the rain.

The night before I'd been out late, drinking with friends.

We'd closed the pubs and then gone on to a nightclub where I'd asked for bourbon, gotten strange looks, and made do with whiskey, straight. I'd woken to the alarm clock sounding as though it were a siren announcing a bombing raid. Coming to the final interview for my Green Card with a hangover was not the wisest thing in the world, I knew. But on the other hand, I didn't want to be fully aware in case something went wrong.

Once again, through the clouds of hangover, I reviewed the possibilities. They were so familiar by now, anticipated so many times over the past year, that the whole scene ran like a movie in my mind with a kind of inevitable smoothness:

The immigration officer calling my name, ushering me into a tiny cubicle, sitting down in a comfortable chair behind his desk and then with a curt wave of his hand indicating that I should sit down too. A small hard wooden chair for me. A supplicant's chair.

He'd be tall, I thought, with a crew cut. Solidly built. A football player in his youth. A churchgoer. A staunch Republican. A man with no time for "persons of exceptional ability in the sciences and arts," the official rubric under which I'd applied for immigration.

The lighting would be strong, unflattering. Probably fluorescent tubes overhead. Even a desk lamp pointed in my direction. Overtones of the third degree.

"And what makes you think we should permit you to become an immigrant to the United States?" he'd ask. Dry and hostile. And I'd sit on the edge of my hard wooden chair, dry mouthed, struck dumb, unable to come up with a single convincing reason.

The trouble was that this vision could hardly be called paranoia. My year's experience with the Immigration and Naturalization Service had made that clear.

The first time I'd met with my immigration lawyer, she'd called me "a sweet case."

"What exactly do you mean by that?" I'd asked.

That question let me in for a half hour of horror stories about immigration cases. Compared to the majority of would-be immigrants, it seemed I was a shoo-in. With any luck, I'd have my Green Card in three months.

I'd filled in form after form after form. One was headed "Statement of Qualifications of Alien," Section 15 of which allowed six lines for "Work Experience." Since I'd been fully employed by a single company for a total of only six months of my life, the pattern of my employment made atomic structure look simple. "I can't fit on this form," I'd said in exasperation.

The lawyer had leaned across the desk, face set in determination, and practically hissed her response. "We will *make* you fit," she said.

Thirteen good American friends had sent letters of recommendation for me, attesting to the fact that I'd be a valuable addition to American culture. "Of course we'd be glad to do it," they'd said, "but why?"

"I don't know," I'd replied. "That's what they want."

American citizens, they were blissfully unaware of the impenetrable intricacies of immigration bureaucracy.

Then, "You have to prove," said the lawyer, "that you're a writer of international repute."

"But why international? Surely it's more relevant if I have some American repute."

"They want international," she replied grimly, "and they'll get international."

Which they did. I dug out old reviews of my books and photocopied press clippings in German, Hebrew, Arabic, Swedish, and French, as well as Australian, British, and Canadian English. "It's a shame there's no Japanese," said the lawyer.

I submitted "background documentation"—photocopies of articles, essays, book jackets, contracts—photocopies of my life, it seemed.

"Perhaps we should send them my bank statements and the deeds to my apartment as well," I said nastily.

"We will," said the lawyer, implacably.

And we did.

All this went to a faceless bureaucracy. The branch of the Immigration and Naturalization Service dealing with immigration visas was up in Saint Albans, Vermont. It had no listed phone number. Not even the immigration lawyers knew the phone number. It also had no address, just a post office box number.

"Are you sure they really exist?" I'd asked.

The lawyer made a face. "They exist," she said grimly. "And how."

I never stopped to count the number of pages we submitted to the Immigration and Naturalization Service, but by my best reckoning the last time I'd seen my file it had been some three inches thick. The size of a large book.

I filled in Form I-140, "Petition to Classify Preference Status of Alien on Basis of Profession or Occupation," which would determine how long I'd have to wait—a few months or a few years—until my case was reviewed. I was lucky; by applying as a professional writer I'd receive priority.

I liked the word petition. It added to the Kafkaesque quality of it all. A petitioner, on her knees, making her way up the long, hard hill to America.

Then I waited for a "priority date" to be established. There was no rational estimate of the time that would take. It depended on the general caseload, on the number of current applicants from England, and on a whole slew of bureaucratic imponderables.

The "sweet case" rapidly became bittersweet. Three months had long passed. Then six. Then nine.

Meanwhile, I filled out the form that would set police checks in motion. Any country where I'd resided for more than six months would be checked. "Who says I couldn't get a criminal record in less than six months?" I asked the lawyer.

She sighed in exasperation. "Who says they have to be logical? Just fill it in."

At last we received permission to fill in Optional Form OF 230, "Application for Immigrant Visa and Alien Registration." I still don't know why it was called an optional form, since it was the one form that was absolutely central to the whole process. But I'd learned something over the preceding months: Don't ask the reason when you know there is none. Just do it and get it over with.

That was not as easy as it might seem. Item 30 on OF 230 asked me to list all the foreign languages I spoke, read, and wrote. There was only room on the form for one language. I squeezed in three in miniscule block letters and wondered what you did if you were Vladimir Nabokov.

Item 49c wanted to know if I was an anarchist or a Communist or sought to engage in any activities prejudicial to the public interest, or if I had ever written anything which might advocate Communism or anarchism or anything prejudicial to the public interest. I hadn't, but this question was courtesy of the infamous Section 212(a) of the McCarran-Walter immigration act, which uses activities protected under the U.S. Constitution as a means of excluding "undesirable aliens." Often, its application seems arbitrary.

At various times, "undesirables" have included Graham Greene, Doris Lessing, Alberto Moravia, Michel Foucault, Czeslaw Milosz, Julio Cortazar, Dario Fo, Gabriel García Márquez, and Pablo Neruda. No specific reason was ever given for their exclusion. As Charles Gordon, a former general counsel to the Immigration and Naturalization Service and author of an eight-volume text on immigration law, has said: "You don't need to call someone a Communist. You don't like them, you don't give them a visa."

I had no reason other than the general paranoia of any petitioner up against a faceless bureaucracy to suppose that the Immigration and Naturalization Service did not like me. I also had no reason to suppose that they did like me. Who could tell if something I'd written might offend them?

And then finally, after ten months, a letter had arrived from the American Embassy in London. It invited me to an interview on July 13. The letter was a cheap computer printout. It was from the Chief of the Immigrant Visa Section, but there was no name and no signature.

My final interview was to be with a nameless person.

THE American Embassy did not look well in the rain. Dark patches of wetness stained the facade. There was no line of people waiting for temporary visas outside. They were probably waiting for a dry day.

At the side entrance, I was told to go to the main entrance. I was impressed—a definite rise in status for those applying for permanent visas. I dashed around the building, through several puddles, and up the main steps where a Marine directed me to a large room on the right.

I stood just inside the door, dripping rain on the corded gray carpet as I caught my breath. This was not what I'd expected. There were no cubicles for a start. And nowhere to sit while you were being interviewed. There were about a hundred people waiting on plastic chairs in a roped-off area in the center of the large room, and one by one, slowly, they were called up to a counter with windows, very like a bank counter. There they stood and clasped their hands in prayer as an immigration officer seated on a raised stool behind the counter examined them and their files.

Everything seemed to be going smoothly except for one window where people came away looking anxious and harried. The officer there was a good-looking man in his thirties—the same kind of Hawaiian good looks as Mets pitcher Ron Darling. But where Darling smiles in public, this man frowned. He glared. He intimidated.

Inevitably, all of the supplicants of the day were watching him in wide-eyed wariness.

An hour or so later there was a long pause after the last person left his window. I saw him frowning over a particularly thick file. He was examining it as though he were a sapper dealing with potentially explosive material.

"It's not my file," I said to myself. "It's not mine."

But I knew it was.

Finally, he slammed the file shut and without even looking up, called my name.

"Just be cool," I said to myself. "Keep your cool."

I got up, tripped over the legs of the person next to me, dropped my purse, banged someone in the back as I bent to pick it up, babbled an apology, and finally made my way, thoroughly flustered, to the counter.

He didn't say a word. He didn't look up. He didn't acknowledge my presence in any way. He started going through the file again. I saw my professional life flip by under his thumb.

"That's me," I wanted to say. "Me! Look, here I am!"

I said nothing and clasped my hands tightly together on the counter in front of me.

"Relax," I said to myself.

"Are you kidding?" myself said back.

Finally he looked up. The frown seemed deeply etched into his forehead. He opened his mouth. I felt my knees dissolve.

He spoke very slowly and very softly. "You know," he said, "there's one thing that makes an immigration officer's life difficult sometimes, and that's overkill."

I did a double take. A slow one as the words sank in. They took their time. And then from somewhere deep down inside me, there began a long surge of blissfully pure relief.

Rolaids has nothing on how I felt right then.

I tried to think of something witty and writerly to say in response, but instead I was grinning stupidly and stuttering an inane apology for overloading his desk. He cut me short.

"Raise your right hand," he said.

I blinked, and raised my right hand.

"Do you swear that everything here is true and correct?"

"I do," I said.

I still couldn't believe how simple it was. I just stood there with my hand in the air.

"You can lower your hand now," he said. I could swear he almost smiled.

"What next?" I whispered.

"You come back in three hours."

"And then?"

He looked at me in surprise, as though everything were perfectly obvious. "Then you'll pick up your permanent residency papers," he said. "Your immigrant visa will be stamped into your passport. You'll carry this file back with you and hand it in at Kennedy together with those papers. You must enter the United States within four months or you have to start all over again."

"That's all right, I'm going back next week," I said.

But he was already frowning over someone else's file. It looked very thin and vulnerable. I wondered if it would make his life easy and what that would mean for the person whose life was in that file.

THE rain was still coming down outside. People hurried by, shoulders hunched and heads hidden beneath umbrellas. Cabs threw up spray, and in the square itself deep puddles had formed on the paths between the lawns and trees.

"Mind how you go now," said the Marine on guard in the foyer of the embassy. "Have a good day."

I smiled broadly. So far as I was concerned, the day couldn't have been better. It had all been so simple! I wandered on down the embassy steps feeling gloriously light, as though someone had just cut the cords binding me to this English soil and I was lifting off, floating out over London, over England, over the people deliberately plashing along puddle-filled sidewalks, over the rain-stained houses and mansions and offices, over the mud of Hampstead Heath and the steeples of the countryside, floating way up, above the rain clouds, to that level of the atmosphere where the sun always shines and the weary transatlantic flier lowers the blind on the porthole and tries to get some sleep to forestall jet lag.

With my umbrella still folded, I went skipping across the road and into the square, leaping over some puddles and into others. Over the sounds of the rain—the splish of the raindrops, the whish of the traffic as it sent up spray, soaking passersby, the gentle drumming that softens the regular city noises—I heard light laughter and realized it was mine.

I'd done it! I'd escaped England over twenty years before, but now it was formal, final. For years, I'd been in the uncomfortable situation of straddling the Atlantic—one foot in the States and one, by definition, still in England. But the Atlantic was too broad and too deep; there was no way to straddle it. The superficial similarity of the cultures demanded that I ally myself definitely with one or the other. And now I had done that. Finally I had both feet firmly on the American side of the ocean.

And suddenly I was standing stock still in the middle of Grosvenor Square. I turned slowly and took in the mansions and the embassy, the rain-soaked brick and concrete facades, and it occurred to me that right then, at that very moment, I should surely be feeling some sadness, some vestige of fondness for England. After all, I'd come from here; if I was leaving, there was something of myself that I'd leave behind too. A tear or two surely—some sadness, some doubt, a last rush of nostalgia for "dear old England."

But the only drops on my cheeks were raindrops, pouring off my hair and over my face.

I shrugged. I'd been watching too much "Masterpiece Theatre" on American public television. It had begun to affect my expectations of my own responses. The scene was perfect: Camera comes in close to the rain pouring down my face, then slowly fades back as that grand old lump in the throat rises, the music swells, and the final credits begin to roll. That's how an American thinks of an Englishwoman leaving England. That's how the English think an Englishwoman should feel. While in reality she skips in and out of puddles and laughs.

This was the country that had made me, true. It was also the country I'd had to leave in order to begin the very American process of remaking myself. I'd never had any doubts about leaving and could never imagine myself living here again. Retirement years in that little Cotswold cottage with honeysuckle vines and roses in the stone-walled garden? I'd much rather a cabin on top of a mountain in Vermont or on the water of Puget Sound; a place with a wild unlimited view, with woods and forests and the grand sense of a whole vast continent behind me.

No more quaint little houses. No more of that dreary restrictiveness, the dour reiteration of what one should or shouldn't do, could or couldn't do, might or mightn't do. This day's work was no mere change of residence; it was a formal recognition of a change of identity. A change from "one doesn't" to "I do." From "one can't" to "I can."

"Goodbye to all that," I kept thinking. That's what Robert Graves called his book about World War One; he wrote it and then spent most of the rest of his life outside England. As had Lawrence Durrell. And Graham Greene. And Christopher Isherwood. And W. H. Auden. And John Berger. And Bruce Chatwin, on long trips. So many modern English writers I admired had left. They'd fled this beclouded island and for the most part kept silent about their reasons, only hinting here and there at a sense of stultification, at a need to escape, as though living in England could only hinder their spirit, clamp down on their words, render them helpless in the midst of the pervasive atmosphere of dampening self-consciousness.

And then the rain found its way down the back of my neck and I ran out of the square, retrieved my car, went back to Hugh and Rosie's, and in thoroughly English fashion took a long hot bath.

TEN days later I handed my file in at Kennedy airport. I was fingerprinted. I thought of joking about it, then looked at the poker face of the airport official and thought better of it. Within three months, he said, my Green Card would be in the mail.

New York life took over, and I'd almost managed to forget that I was waiting for anything when a few weeks later a buff envelope with the imprint of the Department of Justice turned up in my mailbox.

I stood stock still, staring at the envelope as though it might suddenly blow up in my hand.

It's a rejection, I thought. It's a demand for further documentation. A request for clarification. Another form. Another deadline.

I tore it open. There was a plastic card inside, but it wasn't green.

They've sent me the wrong card, I thought.

I examined the wavy brown lines on the white background. I studied the photograph, the name, the date of birth—all mine. That was my signature at the bottom, and the fingerprint in a neat little box on the right-hand side was presumably mine. But best of all, printed across the top in big blue block letters were the words Resident Alien.

I'd never been so happy to be an alien.

Later that night after the champagne bottles had been emptied, I put the card away in a drawer. It was, after all, just another piece of plastic, but it stood for so much. I'd crossed the Atlantic years before, but now that crossing was definite, official. Distance and time are not enough to leave a country behind; there has to be a formal rite of passage, and the Green Card was it. It meant that in another five years, I'd give up my English passport and be formally sworn in as an American citizen. Despite my accent, my childhood, my education, I'd no longer be English.

And yet . . . It took me a long time to go to sleep that night. I lay in bed staring up at intricate patterns of light and shadow—the lights of the city filtered through the slats of the blinds, broken into separate planes by the beams and angles of ceiling and walls. As New York buildings go, mine is an old one. It was built in 1928 as an arts settlement house, a center for immigrants who migrated to the tenements of Manhattan's Lower East Side, where they could learn English and the arts and the new ways of American life. First came Poles and Ukrainians and Russians, and then Italians and Irish, and then Hispanics. I had friends whose parents had studied English in this building.

The intersecting planes of light and shadow seemed to reflect the intersecting planes of my life. Studying them, I saw the paradox that every immigrant learns to live with. You can adopt another country, to be sure, but you can no more reject a native country than you can your family.

I had been English; I would be American. Yet what you have been and where you have been always stay with you. They are part of you—part of the complex tissue of culture and experience and personality and sensibility that make you whoever you are. Even if I no longer had any part in England, it had a part in me.

I woke the next morning to the sound of church bells. Sunday bells pealing across the gentle hills of the English countryside, calling parishioners to the church on the village green. Coming wider awake, I recognized the bells of the copper-spired Ukrainian and Polish churches in the East Village calling to a whole generation of immigrants, grandmothers and grandfathers by now, who'd stayed in the old neighborhood while their children, native-born Americans, had gone elsewhere to make their own lives.

The bells were familiar yet alien music, mine and not mine. All the official documents in the world never resolve the paradox for someone who moves from country to country. I was an immigrant. I was English. I was American.

So be it.